American Environmental History
Part One

Dan Allosso

About the author:

Dan Allosso is currently completing his Ph.D. dissertation in Environmental History at the University of Massachusetts, Amherst. Dan also has an M.A. in Latin American History and a B.S in Agricultural Economics. Before returning to graduate school, Dan spent 25 years in the technology industry, in a variety of sales, marketing, and systems engineering roles in large and small companies.

Dan runs a website for his American Environmental History class at environmentalhistory.us and blogs about Environmental History at EnvHist.net.

ISBN 10: 151358849
ISBN 13: 978-1519358844

For Stephanie, Lucy, Sofie, Gio, and Vivi

Introduction

Environmental History is about looking at the past as if the environment mattered. Not that long ago the world seemed so big and human actions so small that it was easy to ignore our effect on the world around us. Today we understand that people have a big impact on our surroundings. And we're becoming aware that our environment has played a part in our individual lives and in the growth of our cultures. Instead of being just a neutral backdrop, the environment is now recognized as a powerful shaper of human choices. That is, history.

By the environment, I mean everything around us. The natural world, but also the manmade world. Often it's difficult to draw a distinct line between those two. We intuitively feel that wooded suburbs are more natural than the city, and the wilderness even more. But if we look closer we often find that the suburban trees were part of a developer's design, and even wilderness areas are special manmade places that have been deliberately protected or even rehabilitated so they resemble our idea of pristine nature.

The environment is also more than just the green part of the world. Even the most sophisticated urbanite depends for her food, water, and energy on elements of a wider environment she may not be aware of. Nor are we talking only about environmentalists. The most jaded materialist depends on the environment as much as the most dewy-eyed idealist.

If environment is a surprisingly complicated word, so is history. Most Americans live with a set of stories that describe who we are and who we ought to be. These are the civics and social studies lessons we're all so familiar with. Historians recognize that many of these stories are not as true as we'd like to think. A lot of our stories have changed quite a bit over time, as have our reasons for telling them. History isn't just data about the past, it's the stories we tell about the past.

So where does that leave us? American Environmental History, for the purposes of this textbook, means looking at our past with special attention to how our surroundings influenced our opportunities, our choices, and our actions; and to how our actions reshaped our surroundings.

There are two basic elements of looking at a past that includes the environment. First, we pay close attention to the physical world. For example, the shape of the American continents and the fact that they are connected to each other but cut off from the rest of the world has influenced American cultures from their prehistoric beginnings to the present. Landforms and waterways, natural resources and climate have all been key factors in how our society has developed and how it continues to change. Second, we remember that how we think about the environment, like how we think about the past, has changed over time, and that those changes affect our current choices and actions. You don't have to dig too deeply into the headlines to find debates raging over coal mining, oil pipelines, depleted fisheries, and climate change. Our beliefs about the world around us and our role in it are important elements of the competing positions taken by advocates on either side of these important issues.

So our goal is to deal with both events and ideas. But realistically, this is a survey of American Environmental History stretching from prehistory to the present. We're going to spend most of our time on events, especially because the environmental elements of many key events in American History are not well understood. Too often our stories of America devote all their attention to political debates or to the philosophies of elite leaders or founding fathers, and these tales are told against a blank background that isn't part of the story at all. The main goal of this text is to show that it's really not possible to understand our past while ignoring the environment.

In a sense, that simple goal is one of the major ways this American Environmental History text differs from the academic field. When historians study Environmental History, especially in graduate school, we spend a lot more of our time drilling into the details and rarely step back to talk about the big picture. As a result, there are plenty of books out there about particular issues such as the Dust Bowl, Colonial America, Agriculture, or our changing perceptions of Wilderness. I assign chapters from some of these texts to my students. But we've never had a textbook for my college course, because there wasn't a book that covered the whole, big picture.

Until now. This textbook is the content of the course I teach at a major East Coast University. It's designed to give you an overview of American Environmental History, and includes suggestions for further reading and chapter supplements that discuss some of the major sources. The organization is more chronological in the first part and more thematic in the second, when many of the issues we cover begin to overlap in time.

Part One begins thousands of years ago in prehistory and chronologically explores the arrival of the first Americans, European discovery of the Americas, Colonial and Early American history, the western frontier, the Industrial Revolution, transportation, and the green revolution.

Part Two, available soon, explores important issues that arose during America's growth and continue to influence our lives today. Water, mining, energy, city life, country life, farming and agribusiness, and potential limits to growth all have deep roots in our past. Part Two examines these issues and connects the past with the present.

Part Three, available in the summer of 2016, is a study guide for readers and for instructors using American Environmental History in their classes. Based on my college course, the study guide includes my syllabus, the additional readings I assign to my students, discussion prompts, exam questions, and reflections on how my students have reacted to the course material.

So welcome to American Environmental History! There's a lot of material to cover. I've tried to arrange it so it's both concise and comprehensive. Let's get started!

Table of Contents, Part One

This is the story of how people first reached the Americas and what they did when they got here. We'll discuss the regular climate cycles that produce ice ages, and the changes that result. We'll discover Beringia, where the ancestors of Native Americans lived for thousands of years. And we'll talk about the first Americans.

The cultures of the Americas developed separately from their Eurasian cousins for about 12,000 years. In this chapter we explore what happened when Europeans discovered the Americas.

Who came to North America? What did they expect? What did they find? What did they do?

In this chapter we explore the lure of the Western Frontier on colonists and early Americans, and how people began expanding westward from the initial European settlements in North America.

The Industrial Revolution not only changed America's economy and spurred the growth of cities; it changed the way Americans relate to the natural environment. In this chapter we trace changes in our ideas of what the environment is for, and who it's for.

Rapidly improving technology reduced Americans' dependence on natural features of the landscape like rivers and lakes. We explore the building of canals and railroads, steam power and internal combustion, and the development of the global transportation network.

In this chapter we examine the complex relationships between Eastern and Western cities, as centers of production and consumption, and the peripheral lands they depended on for raw materials and consumers.

Although we may not be aware of it, the continued existence of the modern world depends on three minerals. In this chapter we'll explore the history of fertilizer.

Part Two

Chapter One: Prehistory

This is the story of how people first reached the Americas and what they did when they got here. We'll discuss the regular climate cycles that produce ice ages and the changes that result. We'll discover Beringia, where the ancestors of Native Americans lived for thousands of years. And we'll talk about the first Americans.

History is about understanding the past using the best resources available, and as new tools and information about the past become available, history changes. In recent decades, scientific breakthroughs have made it easier to understand the long centuries before people started leaving written records. This new information allows us to look farther back, and we've discovered that what happened long before the beginning of recorded history had a huge influence on our lives today.

A big part of this change in understanding the past, for Americans, is recognizing that our continent's history does not begin with Columbus or even with the Vikings, but with the stories of people who arrived in the Americas ten thousand years before the first Europeans. America's deep past was once thought of as just a prehistory that had no bearing on later events or on the present. As we'll see, that view was mistaken.

Humanity evolved in Africa over a period of about a million years.

When they left their original homelands, early humans first spread over the adjacent continents they could get to on foot, as you'd expect. Over thousands of years, these humans settled nearly all of Europe and Asia. But they didn't reach the Americas, because during those early periods of expansion the Americas were separated by wide, un-crossable oceans. You may be aware that a long time ago the continents were all joined together in a landmass known as Pangaea. This is true, but that ended millions of years before the first humans evolved. By the time people came along, the continents and oceans were pretty much where they are today. The isolation of the American continents and the changes that occurred on them when global climate change allowed humans to finally reach them had a major influence on the beginning of our story.

People Like Us

Human expansion across the continents of Earth must have been an epic story of courage and tenacity. It's too bad it all happened long before the invention of writing, which was only about five thousand years ago, so we can only speculate about what these people felt and thought about their adventures. Luckily, scientists have recently been able to tell us more about the environments these humans faced, and even about the people themselves. So we can now see at least an outline of this prehistoric epic.

The modern humans scientists call *Homo sapiens* have been around for close to two hundred thousand years, and for all that time they have been more or less physically and mentally the same as us. That's an important point to remember. Ancient people lacked writing and other technology we enjoy today, but they had comparable physical and mental abilities. They looked like us and to a great extent they thought like us. A few scientists have even suggested that some prehistoric individuals may have had more highly developed physical and mental abilities than we do. After all, they had to survive by their strength and their wits to a much greater degree than many of us living in luxury today. Prehistoric hunter-gatherers who we once pictured as little more than ignorant cavemen adapted and thrived in conditions we'd have trouble facing even with our technology. A caveman (or cavewoman) might actually have an easier time

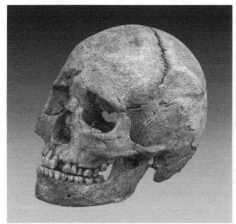

Stone age woman's skull, about ten thousand years old

getting along in our world of WIFI and supermarkets than we would have surviving in his or her world without all the modern conveniences we depend on every day.

The people I'm calling humans in this chapter include a wider variety of folk than you might expect. Until recently, it's been common to reserve the term "human" for only the most recent branch of the evolutionary tree, *Homo sapiens*. It was thought there were extreme and obvious differences between us and our ancestors—that we were in fact different species. But as we learn more about our earlier ancestors, we're discovering they are more like us than we had imagined. Neanderthals, for example, had bigger brains than we do and made stone tools very similar to those made by neighboring *Homo sapiens*.

And these earlier people weren't as isolated from their *Homo sapiens* neighbors as we had thought. One of the biggest discoveries geneticists have made in the past few years is that most modern humans carry genes from people like the Neanderthals and the Denisovans. Since the definition of a species includes being able to breed viable offspring, Neanderthals and early *Homo sapiens* who had children together were clearly much more closely related than we'd once believed them to be. So it makes sense to expand our understanding of humanity to include these people our ancestors mixed with. Maybe we can even learn something from them, as we discover more about their prehistoric lives.

Before 1492

Now consider America. For most people—even for many historians—American history begins in 1492. Everything that happened before Europeans began exploring what we used to call the New World is still often considered to be prehistory. Remote, unknowable, and largely irrelevant. But is it really?

If you happen to be descended from the people who were here before Columbus, you would probably disagree with the idea that American History began in 1492. And actually, outside the United States most of the people in North and South America are descended at least partly from people who were here before Columbus. But even if all your people came to

1842 painting by John Vanderlyn for the U.S. Capitol rotunda, one of countless depictions of Christopher Columbus's 1492 discovery of America.

America on the Mayflower or on a slave ship or passed through Ellis Island, there still are reasons why American prehistory is an important part of your story. We'll explore them in the rest of the chapter, but here are a few highlights:

- *The people who settled the Americas came from the same ancestors as the people who settled Europe. In other words, we're all related.*

- *The people who settled the Americas made one of the epic migrations in the history of our species. So it's a great human adventure.*

- *Early Americans developed three of the five most important foods eaten throughout the world today. So they had a lot to do with making the modern world we live in possible.*

One reason historians often skip over this prehistory is that most of its data comes from other fields of study. It's obviously much harder to know what happened a long time ago, when people didn't leave written records or when those records have been lost. This is a problem not only in the Americas, but throughout the world. Historians have learned to rely on anthropologists, archaeologists, geographers, and linguists to fill in the gaps in their knowledge. And more recently on climatologists, geneticists, geophysicists, and even satellite remote imaging systems to help piece together the stories of ancient peoples and how they lived. As these sciences develop and as new techniques and data become available, our understanding of the remote past can change radically—and sometimes very abruptly. For example, here's the latest on human origins:

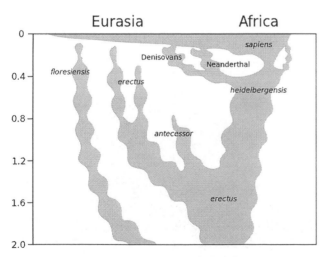

Out of Africa

The most up-to-date data available as I write suggests several waves of human migration out of Africa. The most recent wave—the one that leads directly to us—began roughly 80,000 years ago. Before that, around 150,000 years ago, some type of disaster seems to have reduced the *Homo sapiens* population in Africa to a couple thousand or maybe even just a few hundred people. This time period corresponds with the glacial maximum (the peak of the ice age) before the most recent one, so it's likely that changes in weather patterns altered global patterns of vegetation, reducing the foods available to our ancestors. Scientists aren't sure of the exact cause of the population crisis. What they do know, based on genetic analysis, is we are all descended from those few hundred Africans. The human population recovered gradually and some of the survivors began moving northward from their original homes in Central Africa as climate continued to change, probably following the animals they hunted.

But our *Homo sapiens* ancestors were not the first humans to travel the world. *Homo erectus* left Africa 1.8 million years ago and their descendants were incredibly successful. *Homo erectus* survived in East Asia until about 40 thousand years ago, when they were displaced by migrating *Homo sapiens*. A recently-discovered group called the Denisovans left Africa about 1.2 million years ago. The Denisovans settled in central Asia and contributed a crucial gene to modern people living in Nepal and Tibet that allows their blood to absorb more oxygen in the high altitudes of the Himalayas. The ancestors of the Neanderthals left Africa about 600,000 years ago. They thrived in what is now Europe for more than a half million years, and contributed to the genomes of all modern non-Africans. Neanderthals were unbelievably tough. They survived through several ice ages and only disappeared about 25 thousand years ago when they too were displaced by *Homo sapiens*.

By about 40,000 years ago, a population of *Homo sapiens* hunter-gatherers descended from the people that had survived the African population crisis were living on the Eurasian plains north of the Black Sea. These are your ancestors, if you are Asian, European, or Native American. They used spears, fire, and cooperation to defend themselves from predators, and were experts at hunting huge prey animals like the wooly rhinoceros and wooly mammoth. The Eurasians' ability to adapt to life on the plains and tundra gave them an evolutionary advantage when a new cycle of global cooling extended their habitat across the whole Eurasian land mass from the Atlantic to the Pacific.

Ice Ages

Global climate has been very stable for extremely long stretches of Earth's 4.5 billion-year history, such as during tens of millions of years when dinosaurs roamed the planet. But over the last million years there have been

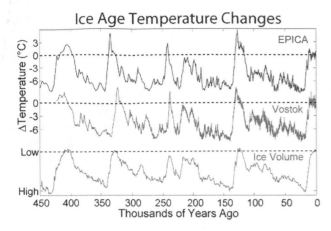

Ice Age Temperature Changes

a series of cyclical climate changes. Over the last 500,000 years (a period we have better data for), global temperatures have varied by about ten degrees Celsius (about 18° F) in a regular cycle lasting around 100,000 years. The highest temperatures were about three or four degrees Celsius higher than now, and the lowest were about six or seven degrees cooler. These are global averages, not local. On a global basis a six-degree Celsius drop in average temperature is enough to bring on an ice age. That's exactly what happened during the cold part of each cycle. Snow fell and didn't melt. Ice accumulated into glaciers that spread northward from Antarctica into the southern oceans and southward from the Arctic Circle to cover most of what is now Europe, all of Canada, and quite a bit of the northern United States. The last time this happened, roughly 36,000 years ago, is when American History really began.

This chart shows the relationship between global temperatures and the Earth's volume of ice. The ice volume line at the bottom is inverted so you can see how ice cover and temperature changes line up. When temperatures fell the ice-pack grew. Notice that about 150,000 years ago, Earth experienced the frigid temperatures of a glacial maximum. That's the climate change that may have caused the population crisis in the African *Homo sapiens* mentioned earlier. As snow became trapped in glaciers, rainfall patterns changed in central Africa, killing plants that had evolved under different conditions. Lack of food reduced the numbers of grazing animals and the humans who hunted them. Later, when the climate warmed, Eurasian glaciers receded and opened new grasslands for the herds, forcing hunters to migrate along with their prey. After expanding across Europe and Asia during tens of thousands of years of mild weather, our ancestors once again faced centuries of cooling and finally another ice age beginning about 36,000 years ago. This climate change created new opportunities as well as challenges.

Glaciers

When global temperatures began to drop slowly at the beginning of the last ice age, the forests of central Europe and Asia died. Trees have a hard time adapting to big changes in climate, and slow-growing forests can't relocate to places with better conditions as easily as other, shorter-lived plants. The Eurasian plains lost their trees and became grassy steppes and then frozen tundra. The onset of the ice age took centuries, and Eurasian hunter-gatherers gradually followed the grasslands and the animals that grazed them. People who would become the first Americans expanded slowly eastward from Central Europe across what is now Siberia, while other members of the same ancestral population expanded slowly westward toward the Atlantic. All these people were the descendants of the survivors who had left Africa between eighty and fifty thousand years ago to live north of the Black Sea.

As glaciers expanded southward to cover Europe and Central Asia, the tundra in the northeastern corner of Siberia stayed relatively ice-free. Ice age weather patterns generally dumped all their moisture in snowstorms over northern Europe, leaving eastern Siberia frigid but dry. The Eurasian plains people adapted to this climate, living in small hunting groups that followed herds of caribou, mammoths, and wooly rhinoceros. These animals provided the hunters with food, hides, and bone tools. The hunters didn't form any large communities we know of, but archaeologists have found the remains of many small camps. A thin, widely spaced population of Siberian hunters held their own in this harsh environment for thousands of years.

By about 21,000 years ago the Earth had reached the coldest point of that glacial cycle. Scientists call this the Last Glacial Maximum—which means only that it was the most recent glacial maximum and is not meant to imply that it was the final one. By the Last Glacial Maximum, the Eurasians had already reached the northeastern edge of Asia. Archaeologists have discovered sites in Eastern Siberia over 35,000 years old. One settlement near the Laptev Sea, called Yana RHS, was occupied 27,000 years ago. The Yana RHS settlement is located within the Arctic Circle at 70° north latitude, near where the Yana River empties into the Arctic Ocean. This is extremely challenging territory even today, but the area may have had a slightly milder climate when Eurasian hunters lived there during the ice age. Excavations at Yana RHS have yielded stone spear-points and shafts of woolly rhinoceros horn and mammoth ivory very similar to objects found at sites in North America. That's because when these hunters got to what is now the edge of Asia, what they found there was not the frigid water of the Bering Strait and Arctic Ocean we'd see today. They found more tundra.

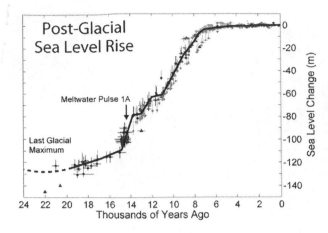

Post-Glacial
Sea Level Rise

Meltwater Pulse 1A

Last Glacial
Maximum

Sea Level Change (m)

0
-20
-40
-60
-80
-100
-120
-140

24 22 20 18 16 14 12 10 8   6   4   2   0
Thousands of Years Ago

Beringia

So much snow fell during the last ice age that glaciers up to two miles thick covered much of the northern hemisphere. Enough water became trapped in those glaciers that many of the world's largest rivers slowed to a trickle or stopped flowing completely. Global sea levels fell by 120 meters (over 360 feet) and coastlines around the world expanded dramatically. For comparison, if all the ice left on Antarctica and Greenland melted, the oceans would rise 60 meters from their current level. This would be a global catastrophe, but it's only half of the sea level change experienced during the last ice age.

The graph above shows sea level changes during the last ice age. Near the left-hand side you can see the last glacial maximum. Sea levels were 360 feet lower than they are today, and people were able to walk from Asia to America. The stretch of ocean that separates Siberia from Alaska isn't very deep. The continental shelf would have been exposed when sea levels had dropped by only about fifty meters. So by the time the Eurasian hunters arrived at the eastern edge of Asia about thirty thousand years ago, the tundra just continued eastward in a thousand-kilometer wide strip of land scientists call Beringia. Although in the past the connection between Asia and America has been described as a "land bridge," the term gives the wrong impression. There was nothing narrow or temporary about Beringia. Worse, the word "bridge" leads us to imagine people deliberately crossing to get from one place to another place. This is a mistake. Beringia was a place. It was nearly as wide as Alaska from north to south and it lasted at least 16,000 years, from about 28,000 years ago until 12,000 years ago. That's three times longer than recorded history. Eurasian plains hunters probably lived in Siberia, Beringia, and in northern Alaska that entire time.

The Eurasians who hunted caribou, mammoths and other big game from what is now Kamchatka to what is now Alaska had no reason to think any differently about the land they occupied. They were following the herds of game animals, living as they had for thousands of years. It's important to understand that the people living in Beringia were not migrating to the new world. If they had been migrating, they probably would have brought more than dogs, which people began domesticating from central Asian wolves about thirty thousand years ago. As far as they were concerned, the Beringians were living the way their ancestors had lived

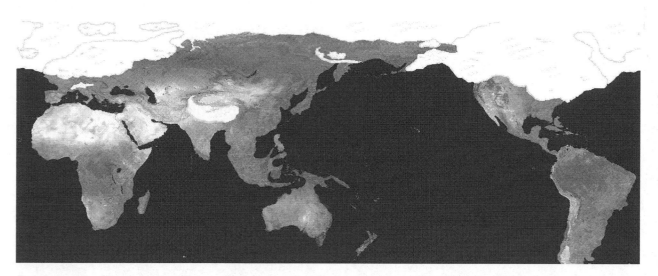

Approximate coastlines and ice-cover at the peak of the last ice age. Note snow-free plains of Western Siberia and Beringia.

for uncounted hundreds of generations.

The most compelling evidence Beringians weren't deliberately migrating into America is genetic. The most recent analyses by paleo-geneticists show there was a period lasting several thousand years, when the ancestors of native Americans paused on the edge of the continent. The likely explanation for this pause is that there was a wall of ice cutting off Beringia from the rest of North America. People living during the ice age would have been very unlikely to climb up onto a two-mile high glacier and try to cross it, even if they knew there was anywhere to go. But beginning about 15,000 years ago, as ice melted and sea levels rose, Beringians would have found themselves gradually cut off from Asia. There was still a narrow strip of land joining the continents until about 11,000 years ago. But the route back to Asia would have been over rougher terrain, former highlands and mountains rather than the wide, flat country the hunters had lived on for so long. The plains the Beringians had spread across had already disappeared under the sea.

Rising oceans created the coastlines of the modern globe and filled the Bering Strait by about 11,000 years ago. The people who expanded from Alaska into North and South America were part of the very sparse population of Beringia. They were not joined by any large migrations of additional Eurasians, although scientists have found evidence of a couple of small migrations back to Asia, when some Beringians returned to Siberia carrying genetic mutations they had developed in Alaska. Based on the most recent DNA evidence, the entire western hemisphere seems to have been colonized from an initial population of fewer than 5,000 Beringians, who entered the Americas in more than one wave. Once they reached the Americas the Beringians (who many historians call Paleo-Indians or Indians, but who I'm going to call Americans) were then cut off from Asia and left isolated by climate change for over 12,000 years.

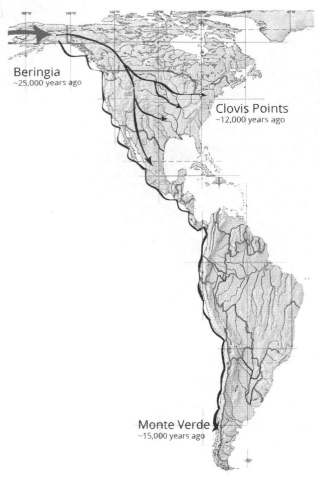

Beringia
~25,000 years ago

Clovis Points
~12,000 years ago

Monte Verde
~15,000 years ago

Into America

As the ice age ended, glaciers slowly melted and retreated northward into the Arctic. But glaciers don't disappear quickly. The two-mile high walls of ice blocking southwestern Alaska began melting on their southern sides in what is now the U.S. and Canada. But they remained a pretty effective barrier in the north. However, on the Alaska coast ocean warming and rising sea levels attacked the edges of the ice, just as they are now doing in Greenland and Antarctica. Scientists don't know exactly when a coastal corridor opened up, or whether Beringians walked south along the water's edge or paddled small boats. What they do know is that by 14,800 years ago, the new Americans had reached the southern coast of Chile and set up camp in a place called Monte Verde.

Southern Chile is a long way from Beringia. The site archaeologists discovered on the banks of a small river is about fifty kilometers from the Pacific coast and about the same distance from Puerto Montt, a small city that stands at the southern end the Pan-American Highway. The other end of the Pan-American Highway is in Prudhoe Bay, Alaska, not far from where the Beringians probably began their journey. The official distance of the Highway between Alaska and southern Chile is just under 30,000 miles. The coastal route curves more than the Highway does; so if you hug the coast the distance is even greater. It may have taken Beringian explorers a thousand years to make the trip. Scientists don't know because they haven't yet found many camps or settlements along the way. One explanation for the lack of archaeological sites could be that rising sea levels at the end of the ice age may have hidden evidence underwater. Recent finds on California's Channel Islands may shed light on the issue—we'll have to wait and see.

Archaeologists at Monte Verde found stone tools and scraps of mammoth and llama hides, log planks, wooden tent-pegs tied with grass twine, and a wide variety of other plant and animal remains. Nearly a third of the plants found at Monte Verde were charred from cooking, which tells us the new Americans who lived there had a varied diet that included a lot of vegetables. About a quarter of the plants archaeologists have catalogued were not from the immediate area, but had been imported to the site. Seaweeds were found stuck to stone tools, that must have been carried from the Pacific coast 50 kilometers away. Other plant foods had been brought from their high-altitude homes in the Andes or from grasslands up to 600 kilometers away. It's interesting that more than half these plants are still used by the Mapuche Indians of southern Chile as food, drink, medicine, or construction materials.

Early Americans were not only incredibly mobile, they were remarkably good at learning which local plants were healthy to eat. This knowledge is even more impressive when we recall that as they traveled southward along the coasts of North, Central, and South America, the Beringians left the arctic tundra environment they knew so well, and passed through strange new ecosystems. The explorers crossed the equator and experienced tropical weather for the first time in a thousand generations. But early Americans were apparently very fast learners. According to a leading archaeologist, no one has ever found a plant native to the Americas with food or medicinal value that was not familiar to the pre-Columbian natives.

Monte Verde was an unusual find for archaeologists. Plant remains almost never last more than a couple thousand years, and even bones are rare at most American sites over a few thousand years old. Stone tools are the most common artifacts found, and scientists have been able to trace the movements of ancient Americans by the types of stone they preferred and the tool designs they left behind. When making their tools, ancient Americans chose high-quality minerals that could be accurately chipped into the sharpest, most durable points. Craftsmen actually traveled hundreds of kilometers to particular quarries. For example, dolomite from the Texas Panhandle shows up in spear points found in northeastern Colorado, 585 kilometers away. Blocks of Ohio chert were carried 380 kilometers to Michigan to be chipped into points and blades.

A Clovis spear-point. This technique of stonework is considered unique to the Americas.

Clovis

The people who made most of the stone spear points found in North America used slightly different techniques from those used by the Monte Verdians. Their style of chipping stone points is distinctive enough that scientists think it represents a new culture in North America, which they called Clovis after the New Mexico town where the first points were discovered in the 1930s. Unlike the first migration of Beringians who traveled down the coast to Monte Verde over fifteen thousand years ago, Clovis

Smilodon, known as the Saber-toothed Cat.

people seem to have followed a land route that opened about 12,000 years ago as the glaciers receded. As the two major ice sheets covering the top half of North America began to melt, a gap opened between them on the eastern edge of the Rocky Mountains. Beringians still living in Alaska would have been able to walk south onto the Great Plains, following the animals that also migrated into the new temperate grasslands. And as the ice sheets melted, sea levels began to rise more rapidly. The land route into North America seems to have opened at about the same time the route back to Asia began to close once and for all.

Archaeologists have found many Clovis sites of about the same age throughout North America, leading them to believe the continent may have been completely explored by Clovis people in as little as 500 years. There's a bit of controversy surrounding the relationship between Clovis people and other groups, because Clovis was discovered first and the discoverers have been reluctant to see Clovis people lose their status as the First Americans. It's unknown, and a source of ongoing debate, how many coastal travelers like those who made the trip down to Monte Verde might have been in the Americas before the Clovis people. But the evidence is mounting that remains like those of Kennewick Man and Hoyo Negro Girl are from people who lived in the Americas before the Clovis culture arrived. Some people have even suggested that small groups may have managed to cross the Pacific from Oceania or the Atlantic from Africa. Although these possibilities can't be completely ruled out, DNA evidence shows that most of the ancestors of the early Americans came through Beringia.

The important point is that after countless generations living as hunters in ice age Siberia, Beringia, and Alaska, early Americans quickly adapted their lifestyles to a variety of new American environments. This rapid change may be related to a dramatic drop in large animal populations called the Holocene Extinction. In just about a thousand years, around the time the Beringians entered the Americas, most of the largest mammal species died out. Predators like the Beringian Cave Lion, the Saber Toothed Cat, the Dire Wolf, and the Giant Short-Faced Bear disappeared. Most of the biggest prey species like the Ancient Bison, the Wooly Mammoth, Mastodon, Stag-Moose, and Western Camel also went extinct. Scientists disagree over whether humans caused the die-off through overhunting the animals, or climate change at the end of the ice age eliminated their habitats. In either case, the continent-wide extinction event had dramatic consequences on the people hunting these animals—and also on people who were hunted by them. The disappearance of these species changed the American environment substantially.

The Hebior Mammoth, discovered in the 1990s in Kenosha, Wisconsin. Its bones are 14,500 years old and show marks from stone tools early American hunters used to butcher the animal.

Luckily for early Americans, there were still plenty of large animals to hunt, even if they weren't quite as big as the ones that had disappeared. The modern bison, although not eight feet tall at the shoulder like its extinct ancestor, still weighs about a ton and its habitat expanded rapidly as ice sheets and melt-water lakes gave way to grassy plains. Smaller quarry for early American hunters included deer, pronghorn, jackrabbits, prairie dogs, and freshwater fish and mussels. The Beringians had brought their dogs with them from Asia, but the only American mammals they were able to domesticate were llamas and their smaller cousins alpaca and vicuña, which they used as pack animals and for their meat, wool and hides. The Americans' lack of large domesticated mammals caused their societies to develop differently from African, European, and Asian cultures that had beasts of burden such as oxen and horses. However, the early Americans quickly found plants they could expertly adapt to their needs.

Agriculture

Farming was once believed to have developed in the Middle East at sites such as Jericho and Mesopotamia six or seven thousand years ago, where the ancestors of modern Europeans (and the men writing the histories) were usually credited with the invention of agriculture. Then, responding to evidence of prehistoric farming in Africa, India, and China, it was suggested agriculture may have developed more or less independently in several regions of the world. But it was difficult to imagine how such parallel development could have occurred, with people in different parts of the world not only making the same basic discoveries but making them pretty much simultaneously. More recently, scientists have begun to suspect this confusion may reflect the difficulty of finding archaeological evidence, since plant materials decay in the ground much more quickly than arrowheads and stone spear points. And some have suggested we may have been thinking about agriculture wrong.

Teosinte (left) was selectively bred over generations into Maize, the most important cereal grain in the modern world.

It now seems likely that agriculture began in a very gradual process that goes back much farther than we had imagined, to a time when hunter-gatherers began favoring certain plants, weeding around them to help them grow, and then transplanting their favorites closer to home. This horticulture or part-time farming may have begun before our ancestors began to spread from Central Europe across Eurasia, which would explain the seemingly coincidental parallel development of farming across the globe. Various regions may have each developed their distinctive versions of what we now recognize as agriculture from a deep pool of common techniques. But whatever the original source of their knowledge, Monte Verdians were already experts at finding and using native plants nearly fifteen thousand years ago. And it didn't take long for their descendants to begin selectively breeding native American plants into some of the world's most important staple crops.

Maize, which we call corn, was developed by Central American natives of what is now Southern Mexico beginning about 9,000 years ago. The Central Americans created the single-stem, large-eared maize plant we're familiar with by very gradually improving a native grass called teosinte. Year after year farmers saved seeds from the best plants with the biggest seed heads. Eventually, after generations of patient improvement these seeds began to look less like grass, and more like what we'd call ears of corn. This process of selective breeding may have taken centuries, and along the way the maize plants lost the ability to reproduce by themselves. Modern corn seeds are trapped on their ears, and most will never germinate unless they're removed by people and replanted. Today, maize is the world's most important food crop. Corn feeds billions of people and domesticated animals and produces a wide range of materials for energy, plastics, pharmaceuticals, and other industries.

Potatoes are even older than corn. Papas, as they're called in the Andes Mountains, were developed by South Americans over the period from 10,000 to 7,000 years ago, in a high-altitude region of what is now Peru and Bolivia. Even today, markets in many Andean villages still sell hundreds of potato varieties people outside the region have never seen. South Americans bred potatoes for a wide range of uses. Farmers were freeze-drying potatoes for long-term storage thousands of years before these techniques were first recorded by Spanish conquistadors. Potatoes were among the first "New World" products carried back to Spain by the conquistadors. They were widely adopted by European farmers and had solved Europe's recurring famine problem by 1900. British economist

Adam Smith called Europe's attention in *On the Wealth of Nations* to the fact that fields planted with potatoes instead of wheat would feed three times as many people. Potatoes remain one of the top five staple foods in the world today.

Cassava trees are native to central Brazil, where they were first domesticated between 10,000 and 7,000 years ago. Although the product of the cassava tree, called manioc, is only familiar to most North Americans as the desert tapioca, the processed roots of this jungle tree are another of the world's top five staple crops. Manioc feeds billions of people in Asia and Africa. But unlike maize and potatoes, the roots of the cassava tree are toxic in their raw form, containing cyanide compounds that must be removed before manioc can be eaten. Processing manioc involves grating, milling, fermenting, drying, and roasting the cassava roots—in various combinations depending on the end-product being produced. So in addition to discovering this food source when they reached Brazil, early Americans had to develop processing technologies to make it useable.

Cassava roots are poisonous before they are processed into manioc.

Early American Cultures

Learning to grow and store plant foods in addition to hunting changed everything in the Americas, just as it had in Europe, Asia, and Africa. Nomadic hunter-gatherers who had always followed herds of prey animals began staying in one place, literally putting down roots with the crops they planted. Abundant, regular food supplies allowed populations to grow. Soon people were building the ancient cities whose ruins still amaze us today. Like their cousins in Egypt, India, and Asia, early Americans built remarkable cities. Tiwanaku, located near the shores of Lake Titicaca in the Bolivian highlands, was built about 3,500 years ago. Its 30,000 inhabitants developed a farming technique called flooded-raised field agriculture and covered the hills around the lake with walled terraces. This was an especially impressive achievement since the Tiwanakans were working at some of the highest

Cliff Palace, Mesa Verde.

altitudes ever inhabited by people. The water level of Lake Titicaca is at an elevation of 12,500 feet; the irrigated hills around the lake rise from there.

In the twelve thousand years they were cut off from the rest of the world, early Americans developed a variety of civilizations. Many of these cultures existed simultaneously and trade networks developed that carried items like Upper Michigan copper, New England seashells, and Minnesota pipestone across entire continents. Cities such as Cahokia in Illinois, Machu Picchu in Peru, Chichen Itza in Mexico, and Pueblo Bonito in Colorado are just a few of the most visible, well-known remains of native cultures. By the fifteenth century, when the Americans would once again encounter their European cousins, the western hemisphere was probably equal to Europe in both population and culture.

Civilizations rose and fell in the Americas, long before the Americans and the Europeans met again in the fifteenth century. The Mississippian culture of North America peaked around 1200 CE, and seems to have collapsed during the Little Ice Age. The Anaasází or Ancient Pueblo culture of southwestern North America seems to have gone into a similar decline during this period of rapid climate change. The Mayan culture of Mexico flourished between about 1800 BCE and 900 CE. There are several theories about Mayan decline, but the consensus seems to include a combination of overpopulation and agricultural collapse, possibly brought on by increased aridity and desertification. In South America, the Inca empire called itself Tawantinsuyu, or four parts together, referring to the four distinct ecological regions the Inca joined together to form the largest empire in pre-Columbian America. And many continuously successful regions such as the territory occupied by the Triple Alliance (Aztecs) in the fifteenth century had been home to earlier cultures such as the Toltecs (800-1000 CE) and Olmecs (1500-400 BCE) that were conquered or absorbed by the cultures that followed.

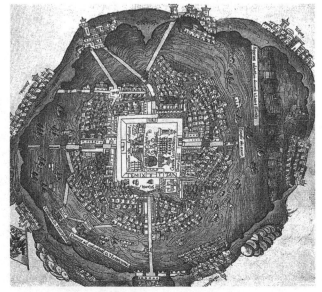

1524 Spanish map of the Aztec Capital, Tenochtitlán, showing Lake Texcoco and the city's many causeways.

The Triple Alliance capitals of Tenochtitlán and Texcoco, in the Valley of Mexico, each had more than 200,000 inhabitants when they were discovered by the Spanish. Tenochtitlán was built on an island in Lake Texcoco, and was connected to the lakeshore by a series of causeways. Each of the Aztec cities was larger when the Spanish arrived in the Americas than Paris, London, Rome, Venice or Lisbon. In 1492, the region surrounding Lake Texcoco contained at least a million people. Mexico City, which the Spanish built on the ruins of Tenochtitlán, was

America's largest city when the Europeans arrived. It remained America's largest city in 1600, 1800, and 2000.

The urban Aztecs had a lot of people to feed. They farmed using what we might now call intensive gardening techniques. The Aztecs surrounded their island capital of Tenochtitlán with raised planting-beds called chinampas on floating platforms in Lake Texcoco. This technique allowed Aztec farmers to carefully control soil fertility and watering. The Aztecs supported fifteen people per hectare using chinampas in the fifteenth century. Chinese intensive farming, the most successful agricultural technique known in Europe and Asia, supported only about three people per hectare at the same time.

There are over ten thousand square kilometers of ancient terraced agricultural fields in South America, many at extremely high altitudes.

Although North America had seen its share of city-building cultures such as the Mississippians who built Cahokia, Central and South Americans were much more urban than their northern cousins. And they radically changed the landscapes surrounding their cities. In addition to the Aztec chinampas surrounding Tenochtitlán, the Incas built over 6,000 square kilometers of terraced farms in the Andes. Surrounding Lake Titicaca in Bolivia there were another 5,000 square kilometers of terraces—rising from the lakeside elevation of 12,500 feet. Dotting the eastern slopes of the Andes were cities like Machu Picchu, which was also surrounded by terraces. Many of these sites have been covered and their buildings and terraces torn apart by rainforest trees over the last five centuries, and only recently rediscovered.

Burial Urn from the Marajoan culture of the Amazon. In a region that was believed to be uninhabitable, archaeologists have found the oldest ceramics in the Americas.

Even more surprising than finding new cites belonging to known American cultures is the recent discovery that some areas where it was never believed the environment could support large populations have hidden completely unknown cultures. The Beni region of Amazonian Bolivia is now believed to have been home to a culture that built raised islands on the river's floodplain. They connected their island homes with miles of causeways. Although the remains of these earthworks survive, it was assumed they were natural formations until just a few years ago when archaeologists dug into them and discovered they were constructed from the broken shards of old pottery. The earthworks and canals

of the Beni still have not been completely mapped.

The Amazon Rainforest was had always been considered extremely inhospitable to civilization. The dense jungle simply couldn't feed enough people, it was argued. And if the rainforest was cut down to make space for farms, the region's shallow soils were almost immediately exhausted. But recently, archaeologists have discovered a city called Marajó which was home to over 100,000 people. Marajó thrived on the banks of the Amazon for a thousand years. Instead of the slash and burn agriculture people currently practice in the Amazon, the Majaroans turned the rainforest into an orchard. According to a recent study, the Majaroans grew 138 crops in the forest, more than half of which were trees. And they fertilized their orchards with a charcoal-based supplement called terra preta, which can still be detected in hundreds of square miles of Amazon soils over a thousand years later.

Meanwhile, In Europe

But what about the other Eurasian plains people who had expanded westward, toward Europe? We'll rejoin them in the next chapter, but one interesting change the ancestral Europeans experienced during their westward trek was, they began drinking milk.

Unlike the Americas, Eurasia was home to several large mammal species that people were able to domesticate. One of these species was the aurochs, a grazing animal like a buffalo that stood about six feet tall at the shoulder. The wild aurochs is now extinct. Although at first it was probably hunted for its meat, aurochs were different from other prey animals. Aurochs were a social species and some would accept humans as the leaders of their herds. The aurochs could be bred in captivity, and they gradually lost their fear of people and allowed themselves to be herded. Over time, in exchange for prime grazing lands and protection from predators, aurochs even allowed themselves to be milked. After hundreds of generations, the wild aurochs became domestic milk-cows.

Aurochs, horses, and deer in 17,000-year old cave paintings, Lascaux, France.

At the same time, some of the people who began keeping cattle developed a genetic mutation that allowed them to digest cows-milk as adults. The ability to metabolize lactose, the sugar compound in milk, after childhood is not shared by most of the world's people. Only Europeans and some Africans can digest lactose. In spite of the fact that cows have been familiar companions since the beginning of recorded history, this is a useful reminder that recorded history covers only a tiny sliver of time. Nearly all of the changes that made Native Americans different from the Europeans they met in the Caribbean in 1492 happened recently, after the Eurasian hunter-gatherers who were our ancestors went their separate ways during the last ice age.

Further Reading

Clive Finlayson, *The Humans Who Went Extinct: Why Neanderthals Died Out and We Survived.* 2010.

David J. Meltzer, *First Peoples in a New World: Colonizing Ice Age America.* 2009.

Charles C. Mann, *1491: New Revelations of the Americas Before Columbus.* 2005.

Supplement: Challenging American History

Now that we've looked at America before its discovery by Europeans, let's consider how this story has been told in the past. As I mentioned earlier, as new information becomes available, history changes, often challenging long-held traditions.

In most older American History textbooks, the story begins in 1492. While some of the archaeological information available today was unknown to earlier historians, many were just not particularly interested in Indians or prehistory. Pre-Columbian America was considered remote, unknowable, and irrelevant. Lately, textbook authors have tried to say something about pre-Columbian America. For example, in the 1987 edition of his classic textbook, *American History*, Richard N. Current devoted four pages to his description of America before Columbus. Current said Native Americans shared a common Asian ancestry that enabled Europeans to think of them all as a single race, although he acknowledged "natives had no reason to consider themselves part of one race or culture." Current described the introduction of old world crops like sugar and bananas that "Indian tribes in time learned to cultivate," but he failed to mention that they had independently developed their own staple crops long before Europeans arrived. Current commented that Indian farming "would often seem crude to Europeans" without explaining that most of the time the Europeans' disdain for native practices arose from their profound ignorance of the environment and climate of the new world.

But that was the 80s, you're thinking. Surely things have changed. Let's see. In his extremely popular and well-regarded 2011 textbook *Experience History*, James West Davidson and his team of co-authors give just three paragraphs to the arrival of humans in the Americas. Davidson calls the people who first settled America "nomads," highlighting the term in one of the textbook's few uses of bold-face type. "Nomads" is a code-word often used in the past to suggest that Indians never had quite the same relationship with the land that whites do, and thus had no claim to ownership of their territories. Many Americans throughout history have called the Indians nomads; a college history textbook should explain the term rather than just repeating it.

Describing pre-Columbian agriculture, *Experience History* says, "pioneers in Mesoamerica began domesticating squash 10,000 years ago." But in spite of this, the text claims most Indians were simple hunter-gatherers who "continued to subsist largely on animals, fish, and nuts, all of which were abundant enough to meet their needs and even to expand their numbers." Davidson characterizes the Adena and Hopewell cultures as "peoples who did not farm," in spite of the fact they lived in cities of tens of thousands of people. He explains that Indians didn't learn to farm in the Pacific Northwest because "Agriculture was unnecessary in such a bountiful place."

Davidson does mention the fact that the modern world's most important food crop, maize, was developed by Indians – but this is how he explains it:

Modern-day species of corn, for example, probably derive from a Mesoamerican grass known as teosinte. It seems that ancient peoples gathered teosinte to collect its small grains. By selecting the grains that best suited them and bringing them back to their settlements, and by returning the grains to the soil through spillage or waste disposal, they unintentionally began the process of domestic cultivation.

The problem with this description, beside the fact that it portrays early farmers as bumbling idiots, is that in spite of being written only a few years ago it isn't based on the abundant archaeological information available about early American agriculture. There's no doubt that corn comes from teosinte. That's clear from the plant's genome. And Davidson suggests that a multi-generational process that changed teosinte, a self-seeding native grass, into maize, a hybrid that needs humans to plant it, was an accident. This claim is ridiculous and obscures the fact that ancient Americans knew what they were doing and had the long-term cultural capital to do it.

Experience History does its best to trivialize early America's contribution to modern agriculture. In spite of admitting that "plants domesticated by indigenous Americans account for three-fifths of the world's crops" today, Davidson manages to make it seem like that's no big deal, and was almost an accident. Davidson's discussion of ancient American farming ends with a chart of the "Place and Timing of Pioneering Plant and Animal Domestications." Southwest Asia tops the list, with the development of wheat, peas, olives, sheep and goats. All these developments are dated to 8500 BCE. Next comes China, with rice, millet, pigs and silkworms, dated 7500 BCE. New Guinea and the African Sahel are next, followed finally by Mesoamerica and the Andes & Amazonia, which produced corn, beans, squash, potatoes, manioc, turkey, llamas, and guinea pigs "by 3500 BCE," which is nearly six thousand years after archaeologists date the development of maize, potatoes, and cassava. At best, this is an error that a reputable team of historians should never have let slip into their textbook. At worst, it's a throwback to Eurocentric histories of an earlier era that tried to minimize the tragedy of colonialism by suggesting there was really not much happening in the Americas before Columbus.

Davidson concludes his coverage of pre-Columbian America by observing that "a few centuries before European contact…the continent's most impressive civilizations collapsed." Davidson says the "sudden" and "mysterious" disappearance of cultures like the Mayan, Olmec, Mogollon, Hohokam, Anasazi, and Cahokian was due to "a complex and still poorly understood combination of ecological and social factors." In other words, through some combination of ecological mismanagement and social ineptitude, Indians "went into eclipse by the twelfth century…[and] had faded by the fourteenth," making room for whites from Europe. That's a bit too convenient. It almost seems like Boston theologian Cotton Mather's famous explanation in *Magnalia Christi Americana* of how Providence had cleared the woods "of those pernicious creatures, making room for better growth."

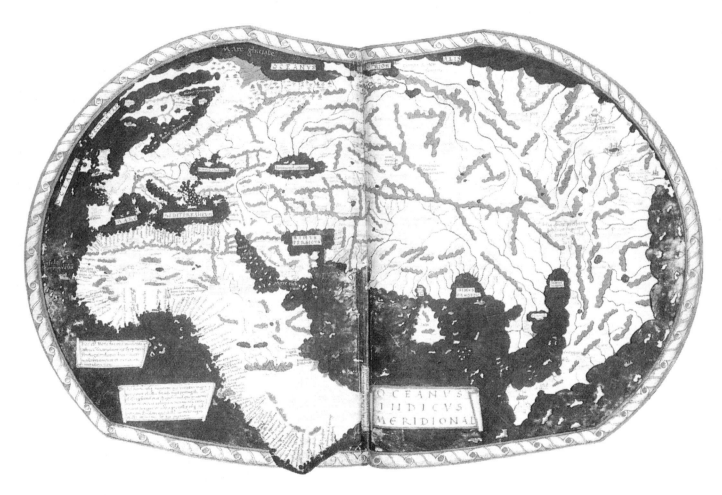

This 1490 German map of the known world indicates why Columbus thought he could reach Asia by sailing west. Most Europeans were unaware there were continents in the way.

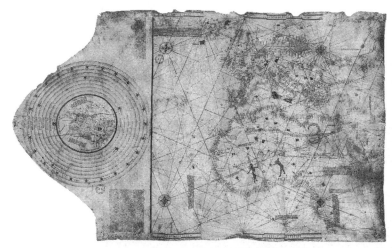

Map of the known world from the workshop of Bartolomeo and Cristoforo Colon (Columbus), 1490.

Chapter Two: Re-contact

The cultures of the Americas developed separately from their Eurasian cousins for about 12,000 years. In this chapter we'll explore what happened when Europeans discovered the Americas.

We all learned as children that Columbus discovered America on October 12, 1492. But as we discussed in the last chapter, important human interactions with the American environment had been going on for millennia when Europeans first made their way to the "New World." In recent years, some historians have retold the traditional story of European exploration with an emphasis on the brutality of groups like the conquistadors. Indian activists have called for boycotts of Columbus Day and Thanksgiving. Our goal here is not to choose sides, but to recognize environmental factors that influenced the course of events. Some of these factors were introduced in the last chapter. The shapes and placement of continents on our planet, and the climate changes surrounding the ice ages influenced the development of civilizations in both Eurasia and the Americas. In this chapter, we'll examine how less obvious environmental factors such as the distribution of animal species and the ways humans changed when they first domesticated animals also had a major impact on history when Europeans began sailing ships across the Atlantic Ocean.

As you're probably already aware, the 2 AM arrival of Christopher Columbus's little fleet of three ships in the fall of 1492 has been frequently challenged as the first contact between Europeans and the Americas. Some claims of first contact are better supported by evidence than others. One of the best documented happened nearly five hundred years before Columbus's arrival.

Vikings

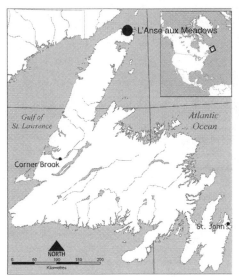

At the northern tip of Newfoundland, there's a Canadian Provincial Park called L'Anse aux Meadows built on the site of a Viking settlement. The Norse have an old legend that Viking hero Leif Erikson founded a colony in a new land they called Vinland. The discovery of the Norse village in 1960 and its acceptance as a UNESCO World Heritage site in 1978 established the Newfoundland colony as the oldest known European site in the Americas, and very probably as the Vinland settlement of Norse legends. The Canadian ruins date from the appropriate period, around 1000 CE. Artifacts found in the remains of eight buildings include farm implements and blacksmith tools. There is also a spinning room containing a soapstone spindle and stone weights that were probably part of a loom. The presence of these artifacts suggests the settlement probably included women, and possibly even families. In other words, the Newfoundland site seems to have been a permanent colony rather than merely a seasonal fishing camp. It was probably an extension of the permanent Viking settlements on Greenland that were the home of Leif Erikson's father, Erik the Red.

Norse legends say the Vinland colonists were attacked by vicious natives the Vikings called Skraelings, suggesting the native Newfoundland population resisted the newcomers fairly effectively. This map, drawn in 1570 in Skálholt, Iceland, shows Great Britain on the bottom right, Iceland in the center, and on the left Grönlandia (Greenland), Helleland (the land of flat stones), Markland (the land of forests) and Skraelingeland, which a note in the text says was close to Vinland (the land of meadows). The forests of Markland would have been especially interesting to explorers from Greenland, because the Norse settlements there lacked trees for building.

The scarcity of additional Norse sites and the fact that we're not all speaking Norwegian remind us that the Vikings failed to sustain their settlement in Vinland. While we can probably attribute this failure partly to the resistance of the Skraelings, another decisive factor was a change in global climate. In the middle of the fourteenth century, a four hundred-year period of global cooling known as The Little Ice Age began. Scientists have measured the effects of this climate

change in tree rings as far away as Patagonia. Changes in temperature and weather were noticed and recorded in Mayan and Aztec Chronicles, and also in European paintings depicting Londoners drinking, dancing, and skating on the frozen Thames. Pack ice in the North Atlantic expanded southward, making travel to America much more difficult and dangerous. Greenland's glaciers advanced and shortened growing seasons threatened the five hundred year-old Viking settlements there. By the early 1400s the Norse had abandoned these settlements, and without Greenland it was impossible to sustain a colony in Vinland. This 1747 map of Old Greenland mentions that the coastline where settlements had once been located had become "inaccessible" due to "floating and fixed mountains of ice." The map even includes the location of a legendary strait that was believed to have once allowed travelers to sail through the center of the continent to North America, but had become "shut up with ice." It's interesting to speculate what American history would look like today, if the Vikings hadn't been defeated by Skraelings and climate change.

Fishermen

Even during the Little Ice Age, Europeans continued to venture into the icy Atlantic and many probably sailed most of the way to the new world. Basque fishing fleets, for example, began crossing the North Atlantic to visit the Grand Banks in the middle of the fifteenth century. The Banks are areas of shallow water on the edge of the North American continental shelf which are warmed by the Gulf Stream. These warm, shallow waters are an ideal home for bottom-dwelling species like Cod and Lobster. Whoever first discovered the rich fisheries of the Grand Banks off Newfoundland and Georges Bank off Cape Cod, by the late 1400s thousands of Europeans were crossing the ocean to take advantage of the bounty. Venetian explorer Giovanni Caboto (who Anglicized his name to John

Cabot) reported in 1497 that Grand Banks cod were so abundant that you could almost walk across the water's surface on their backs.

Cod had been fished in the North Atlantic at least since the period of Viking exploration, 800 to 1000 CE. The Vikings and the Basques used similar techniques, catching fish close to shore and then drying them on wooden racks assembled on nearby beaches. They probably landed regularly on the coastlines near the fishing grounds, to dry fish and to replenish their supplies of fresh water. While the locations of prime fishing grounds were closely-guarded trade secrets, by the late 1400s the Portuguese had found out and had begun sending their own fleets to the Grand Banks. Salted Cod is still an important element of Portuguese cuisine, although nowadays they get their fish from Norway.

Until their defeat as part of the Spanish Armada in 1588, Portugal was a North Atlantic naval power. And in the early 1480s, Christopher Columbus was a sailor on the West African coast, where he regularly visited the Portuguese trading post at Elmina. Columbus's home base was in Lisbon, and his wife was Filipa Moniz Perestrelo, the daughter of the Portuguese governor of Porto Santo, an island off the Atlantic coast of North Africa. It's very possible that Columbus first heard of the new world from Portuguese sailors retelling the stories of Basque fishermen.

By the end of the fifteenth century, Europe was recovering from the Black Death that had killed between 100 and 200 million people 150 years earlier. Fish from the Grand Banks helped feed growing populations, and Europe entered a period of economic and cultural growth we know as the Renaissance. Merchants were reminded of the existence of wealthy empires in India and China, and began taking advantage of trade routes such as the Silk Road. German blacksmith Johannes Gutenberg developed a printing press, which allowed Christopher Columbus to read *The Travels of Marco Polo* as a young man in Genoa. The Italian learned to sail and became a navigator working the Atlantic coast of Africa. In 1492 Columbus convinced the monarchs of a newly unified Spain to finance a mission to discover a sea-route to China. King Ferdinand of Aragon and Queen Isabella of Castile had just combined their kingdoms and their armies, and after nearly 800 years of war had driven the Muslims out of the Iberian Peninsula. It's worth remembering that the new Spanish nation that turned its attention to exploration in 1492 had been at war constantly since the dark ages.

As you'd expect, it's very difficult to be certain about the exact population of the world

Christopher Columbus's copy of The Travels of Marco Polo, with his handwritten notes in the margins.

at the end of the fifteenth century. There are a number of competing estimates, but the consensus is that there were probably about 500 million people alive in 1492, and that slightly over a third of them lived in Asia. The other two-thirds seem to have been about evenly split between Europe, Africa, and the Americas – although there's still a great deal of controversy surrounding those numbers. Even so, if we take a conservative number from the middle of the range of estimates, we get an American population of 80 to 100 million just before Columbus and his fellow explorers arrived. All but 2 or 3 million of those Native Americans lived in Central and South America, which were much more densely populated than North America.

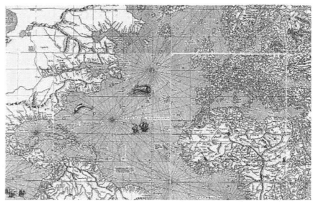

Detail from Gerardus Mercator's 1569 world map. Note the lines crossing the oceans. The map was optimized for sailors, to show ocean distances and directions as accurately as possible.

Maps and Bias

You may have noticed I've already used several different maps of the world, and the continent shapes of some of them may seem a bit unfamiliar. It's always tricky, translating the features of a spherical planet onto a flat surface. A number of different projections have been used, and each has its benefits and drawbacks. The map I prefer in this text is called a Gall-Peters Projection. Unlike the maps you see in most books and classrooms, the equator is actually in the middle and the sizes of the continents and countries are true to scale.

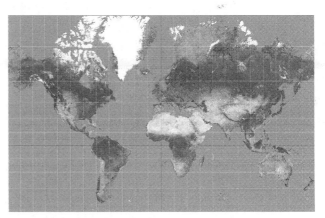

Modern world map based on Mercator projection. Continent sizes are inaccurate and the Northern Hemisphere takes up the top two thirds of the map.

The standard map projection, which was developed in 1569 by Gerardus Mercator, is better for measuring point to point distances. This was very important to the sailors who were Mercator's customers. But the Mercator projection is notoriously bad at displaying the shapes and sizes of continents. Mercator himself was aware of this problem, but getting the ocean routes right was so much more important that he and his cli-

World map based on Gall-Peters Projection. Continent sizes are accurate and the equator is in the middle.

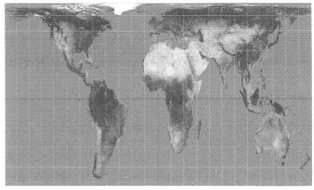

ents put up with the errors. Africa and Greenland, for example, seem to be the same size on a Mercator map, when in fact Africa is fourteen times bigger than Greenland.

Why then is the Mercator map still so widely used? Although there are some slight regional variations, in Europe and the Americas most maps are still drawn using a Mercator projection with the Europe in the center. Mercator was a Flemish merchant and his clients were European sailors. So Europe is prominently in the Mercator map's center and the northern hemisphere gets more than its fair share of space. But fast forward five hundred years, to a time when most map users are neither sailors nor Europeans. If we continue to imagine Europe, and indeed the whole northern hemisphere, as much bigger than it actually is, and the "developing world" as much smaller, does that influence how we think about the relationships between these regions? What does it say about our own unexamined biases, that we're still using a map that distorts the world so extremely, and we don't even know it?

The Columbian Exchange

Columbus arrived in the Caribbean in October 1492 and explored until late December. His flagship, the Santa Maria, ran aground on Hispaniola on December 25th and had to be abandoned. With permission of the local chief, Columbus left 39 sailors behind in a settlement he named La Navidad. He returned to Europe with two ships, a few Indians, some gold, and specimens of native species including turkeys, pineapple, and tobacco. Arriving in Barcelona in mid-March, Columbus was celebrated as a hero.

It is often mentioned that Columbus believed he had reached Asia, and he did make that claim in his extravagant "Letter on the First Voyage." But this letter was the explorer's report to his royal sponsors, and he wanted very badly to be sent back again. Columbus wrote "Hispaniola is a miracle...both fertile and beautiful...the harbors are unbelievably good and there are many wide rivers the majority of which contain gold." Whether or not Columbus understood he was reporting on previously unknown lands, he definitely got people excited about the places he had visited.

When other European explorers reached America they were equally amazed. People throughout Europe read exciting traveler's ac-

Columbus made four trips to the Caribbean, in 1492, 1493, 1498, and 1502.

counts like Amerigo Vespucci's 1504 best-seller, *Mundus Novus*, which actually coined the term New World and made it clear for anyone who might still be confused, that these lands were not Asia but a previously unknown continent. Like Columbus, the explorers carried back to Europe not only stories of wealthy civilizations and legends of cities of gold, but samples of native plants, animals, and captive Indians. And when Columbus himself returned to the Caribbean, he brought with him European plants and animals that he transplanted into the promising new environment.

Red Jungle Fowl hen, native of Indonesia, ancestor of all chickens.

Europeans realized not only that American food crops could be brought back to Europe, but also that the Americas were a great place to grow many of Europe's traditional foods. Columbus returned to the Caribbean in 1495 with 17 ships, 1,200 men, and according to his diaries, "seeds and cuttings for the planting of wheat, chickpeas, melons, onions, radishes, salad greens, grape vines, sugar cane, and fruit stones for the founding of orchards." Other old-world crops that thrived in the Americas included coffee and bananas, which were brought from the Canary Islands in 1516. The Spanish had introduced sugar cultivation to the Canary Islands in the early fifteenth century, so it only made sense to try the plant in the tropical paradise their explorers had discovered across the Atlantic. Cattle were delivered to Spanish conquistadors in Mexico in 1521. By 1614, according to one of the conquistador chronicles, "the residents of Santiago [in Chile, over 4,000 miles away] possessed 39,250 head," as well as flocks totaling 623,825 sheep. According to local traditions, when Pizarro first invaded Peru in 1524, he crossed the Andes with only eighty fighting men and forty horses, but with over 2,000 pigs.

Most of the really significant Eurasian species brought to the Americas had already been introduced by the Spanish by the early 1500s, long before North American settlement began. Even species like the wild horses of the American West that would transform Plains Indian culture were escapees from the herds of the conquistadors. As mentioned earlier, the Americas were home to very few large mammal species, and most could not be domesticated. Domestication is only successful with social animals that will accept a human as the leader of their herd or pack. Nearly all the species humans have successfully domesticated, the familiar residents of the modern farmyard, originated in Europe and Asia. These include goats, sheep, cows, horses, pigs and chickens. Eurasians began domesticating these animals between ten and fifteen thousand years ago. This was just a little too late for the Beringians to bring domesticated

The Variola virus, which causes smallpox.

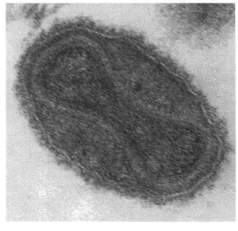

animals with them into North America. In any case, the Beringians were tundra hunters, not temperate-zone pastoralists. But as any good hunter would, the Beringians had brought their dogs.

Historians call the transfer of plants and animals that began with fifteenth and early-sixteenth century European-American re-contact the Columbian exchange. The directions of these transfers and their effects on the environments and people of Europe and the Americas shaped the modern world we live in. American maize, potatoes, and cassava fed growing European and Asian populations, allowing the building of new cities and industries. European animals such as pigs, sheep, chicken, and cattle thrived in the Americas, allowing both Natives and Europeans to expand and change their cultures. But the most significant change of all was the largely accidental transfer of viruses and bacteria from Europeans to Americans, which caused the deaths of possibly 90% of the native American population.

When prehistoric Eurasians began living in close contact with the species they domesticated, the people changed as well as the animals. We've already noted how Europeans and some Africans developed a mutation that allowed them to digest cows-milk. Another change domesticated animals brought to humans, which was largely unrecognized by historians until recently, was disease. Most of humanity's major diseases originated in animals and crossed from domesticated species to their human keepers. Whooping cough and influenza came from pigs; measles and smallpox from cattle; malaria and avian flu from chickens. The people who domesticated these species and lived with the animals for generations co-evolved with them. Animal diseases became survivable when people developed antibodies and immunity. Without inherited this protection, even a routine childhood disease such as chickenpox would be devastating.

Aztecs infected with smallpox, from the Florentine Codex, 1540.

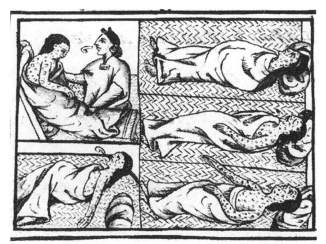

Population Disaster

The introduction of a disease into an area without immunity is called a virgin soil epidemic. Such epidemics had happened in Eurasia, when the Romans spread smallpox into the populations they conquered, and in Europe when the expanding Mongols introduced bubonic plague. The Black Death killed probably half the population of Europe in the fourteenth century, reducing world population by over a hundred million. Virgin soil epidemics happened in the Americas when explorers and colonists introduced Eurasian diseases to native Americans who had been isolated for thousands of years. The Americans had no immunities, and even diseases that were no longer deadly to Europeans killed millions. The Eurasian diseases that attacked native populations included smallpox, measles, chickenpox, influenza, typhus, cholera, typhoid, diphtheria, bubonic plague, scarlet fever, whooping cough, and malaria.

The impact of these Eurasian diseases on Americans was one of human history's most severe population disasters. Even the Black Death didn't kill as large a percentage of Europeans. For example, there were probably a million people living on the Caribbean island of Hispaniola in 1492 when the Columbus left his 39 sailors in La Navidad. By 1548, there were only 500 Natives left alive. The populations of other Caribbean islands were similarly wiped out. Whole civilizations disappeared, but this was not only a tragedy for the cultures that vanished. It began a cycle of violence that became central to American history. Because once there were no natives left to work on European sugar plantations, African slaves became crucial to the survival of the West Indies economy.

The greater population densities of Central and South America helped contagious diseases spread more quickly there. Heavily traveled roads in central Mexico actually spread disease beyond the areas that had been reached by Spanish explorers. Cities were wiped out that had never seen a white man. The population of the Aztec heartland dropped from about 25 million on the eve of the Spanish conquest in 1519 to just under 17 million a decade later. That means one out of every three people died in just ten years. After another decade the Aztec population was reduced to about 6 million. Three out of four people in the Aztec world disappeared in 20 years. Imagine writing a list of all the people you know, and then randomly crossing off three out of every four names.

By 1580, the Aztec empire had been hollowed out to less than 2 million people, from a starting point of 25 million. Isolated rural communities may have been a little luckier

The Aztec Triple Alliance in 1519, just before the Spanish arrived.

The Inca ruler, Huayna Capac, died of smallpox in 1527, five years before Pizarro's army crossed the Andes.

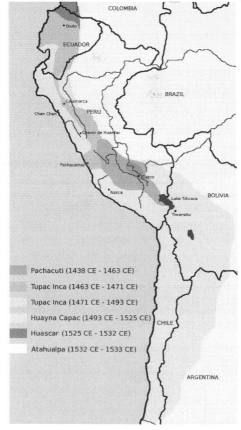

Pachacuti (1438 CE - 1463 CE)

Tupac Inca (1463 CE - 1471 CE)

Tupac Inca (1471 CE - 1493 CE)

Huayna Capac (1493 CE - 1525 CE)

Huascar (1525 CE - 1532 CE)

Atahualpa (1532 CE - 1533 CE)

Peruvian cinchona bark was the source of quinine, which cured malaria and allowed Europeans to extend their colonial empires in the tropics.

than central cities on trade routes, which were often completely emptied. The city of Zempoala, for example, held 100,000 Aztec citizens in 1519. There were only 25 native inhabitants in 1550.

The Inca Empire in the Andes suffered the same fate. 90% of the South Americans died, and they started dying before the white men arrived, which caused confusion and dismay. When Pizarro crossed the Andes with his eighty conquistadors and 2000 pigs, he found social chaos. Huayna Capac, the Inca leader who had extended the empire into Chile and Ecuador, had died of smallpox. His two sons fought a brutal civil war for control of the empire, the younger son Atahualpa finally defeating and assassinating his older brother Huáscar. The war and the weakness of the reduced Inca population gave Pizarro the opportunity he needed to capture and kill Atahualpa in 1533, ending the Inca empire.

Hernando De Soto landed an expedition in Florida in 1539 and explored territory now in the states of Georgia, South Carolina, North Carolina, Tennessee, Alabama, Mississippi, and Oklahoma. Everywhere he went, the conquistador reported the land was "thickly settled with large towns." De Soto didn't stay. He died of fever in Louisiana in 1542, and the region wasn't visited again by Europeans until the French aristocrat, La Salle, traveled down the Mississippi River in 1670. Where De Soto had seen fortified towns, La Salle saw no one. The entire region was empty, and the French explorer traveled hundreds of miles without passing a single village.

The destruction of native empires and the rapid disappearance of the American population was unplanned. The overwhelming success of the conquistadors was an unanticipated consequence of re-contact between two isolated descendant groups of the Eurasian plains hunters we discussed in Chapter One. Sixteenth-century Europeans had virtually no understanding of the causes of disease. They had no idea that exploring the Americas or carrying their animals to the New World would eliminate nine out of ten people in a population that had been the size of Europe's. But they knew how to take advantage of their enemy's misfortunes. The rapid destruction of American populations and cultures created opportunities for Europeans to colonize the Americas that they wouldn't have otherwise enjoyed. We'll take a closer look at this colonization in Chapter Three. But in the meantime, what happened to Europe?

Pieces of Eight

As previously mentioned, American staple crops were introduced in Europe, where they sparked a population boom. Many plant species developed by Americans are still crucial to the world economy, including not only maize, potatoes, and cassava, but tomatoes, sweet potatoes, cacao, chili peppers, natural rubber, tobacco, and vanilla. Quinine, a medicine made from the bark of the Peruvian cinchona tree, was effective treating malaria and helped open the tropics to European colonization. Eurasian plants like sugar, soybeans, oranges, bananas, and rice (which probably reached America from Africa along with enslaved women who were experts growing it) were also extensively cultivated in the Americas for shipment back to European markets. Exports of native and transplanted crops helped feed growing cities and freed up workers for Europe's new industries. Without American foods, there might have been no European industrial revolution.

The other American product rapidly sent across the Atlantic to Europe and across the Pacific to Asia was money. Although Europeans never found El Dorado, the legendary Indian city of gold, they did find a fair amount of gold. And they found even more silver. For example, the Bolivian city of Potosí, located in the Andes mountains at an elevation of 13,420 feet, is said to be the world's highest city. Potosí was established by the Spanish in 1542 on the site of a long-standing native mining village at the foot of the Cerro Rico, which is a literal mountain of silver. Potosí has a current population of about 165,000. That's almost identical to Potosí's population in 1660, when the mining city was larger than Seville, Madrid, or Rome, and when the combined population of all the North American colonies was only about 75,000. Spanish silver coins often called "pieces of eight" from the Cerro Rico and similar mines in Zacatecas, Mexico, were so plentiful that they became the international currency of Europe and much of Asia. Once again, without the money minted in

The first image of Potosí published in Europe, 1553.

16th century painting of the castas, racial classifications of the Spanish colonies.

Latin America, there might have been no global commercial boom to finance the industrial revolution. And Potosí's story isn't over yet. Although most of the silver was taken out of the mountain centuries ago, the Cerro Rico is still being worked by Bolivian children whose story is told in the award-winning documentary, *The Devil's Miner*, which you can view on the web if you're interested in learning more.

As a result of the Columbian exchange, European colonists in the Americas frequently found fields waiting for their farmers and herds of game animals waiting for their hunters. In Central and South America, the Spanish built cities like Mexico City and Cusco right on top of the native cities they replaced. Since Spanish colonists were generally soldiers and very few Spanish women came to the early colonies, there was a lot of racial mixing. Most of the countries of Latin America are built on mixed or mestizo populations; so much so that it became important for the colonists to try to make distinctions between all the various types of people they believed made up their societies. Although these distinctions were initially used to uphold the power of the group at the top, in the long run many of these Euro-American populations have developed strong ethnic identities. A similar process happened to our north, in New France. There were only about twenty-five hundred French people in Quebec by 1663. Most of them were voyageurs, fur traders who went into the northern forests to make their fortunes. Voyageurs married local Indian women, and their Canadian descendants are now recognized as a distinct ethnic group called Métis.

In the Dutch and English colonies that became the United States, the races kept mostly separate. Many settlers migrated with their entire families to settle the British colonies. But the racial segregation that developed in the colonies that became the United States was not inevitable. If the people who had settled the US had mixed more with the natives, genetically and culturally, would our culture and our relationship with our environment have been different?

Further Reading

Alfred W. Crosby, *The Columbian Exchange: Biological and Cultural Consequences of 1492*. 1972.

Charles C. Mann, *1493: Uncovering the World Columbus Created*. 2011.

Shawn William Miller, *An Environmental History of Latin America*. 2007.

Supplement: Changing History

History changes when new evidence and new interpretations challenge long-held beliefs. But the process isn't always easy. Historian Alfred W. Crosby first addressed the idea that disease was a factor in American history in a 1967 journal article called "Conquistadors y Pestilencia." Crosby later said he "stumbled into environmental history through the backdoor of epidemiology." Of course, there was no such field when he wrote, and Crosby helped create it.

"Conquistadors y Pestilencia" re-examines the Spanish conquest. "How did Hernán Cortés do it?" Crosby asked. "Well, he didn't. Old World smallpox did."

"When the isolation of the Americas was broken, and Columbus brought the two halves of this planet together, the American Indian met for the first time his most hideous enemy – not the white man or his black servant, but the invisible killers which these men brought in their blood and breath," Crosby wrote in 1967. Over then next couple of years, Crosby expanded the article into a book whose title became the accepted name of this phenomenon: *The Columbian Exchange.*

Crosby tried for several years to interest publishers in his radical thesis, without success. He sent the manuscript to a dozen academic presses. The most memorable rejection letter Crosby received consisted of a single word, "Nonsense!" Crosby finally landed an unlikely publisher in 1971 when an antiquarian reprint press asked if he had anything book-length he'd like to see in print. *The Columbian Exchange* was published in 1972.

Reception of the book was favorable, although some of the reviewers failed to grasp Crosby's point. One review in a major historical journal described disease decimating both old world and new world populations. Crosby didn't say this, and it wasn't true of the biological exchange he was writing about. Epidemics had indeed decimated European and Asian populations in the past. But not following 1492. The only disease that may have crossed from the new world to the old, Crosby had claimed, was syphilis. Although a killer, syphilis wasn't immediately fatal, and it did nowhere near the damage to Europe that smallpox, plague, and other Eurasian diseases did to native American populations.

Over time, Crosby's thesis attracted historians interested in biological and ecological issues, and *The Columbian Exchange* became one of the founding texts of a new field. Unlike mainstream historians, many of whom rejected the pessimistic conclusion of Crosby's book, environmental historians were willing to consider the possibility that the Columbian exchange was not over. Crosby claimed the events of the sixteenth century were "simply an early phase in a slide toward worldwide biological homogeneity," and that this process is "continuing, even accelerating."

An artist's conception of the First Thanksgiving.

Chapter Three: Colonial North America

Who came to North America? What did they expect? What did they find? What did they do?

The first European nations to establish themselves in the Americas in the sixteenth century were Spain and Portugal. Between the 1490s, when exploratory missions began in earnest, and 1588, when the Spanish Armada was defeated by the English navy, the Iberians ruled the Atlantic. As already discussed, Christopher Columbus was working for the Spanish when he established the first Euro-American settlement since the Vikings at La Navidad in 1492. His brother Bartolomeo founded Santo Domingo, also on Hispaniola, in 1496. In 1500, settlements were begun at Nuevo Cádiz and Santa Cruz, in what is now Venezuela. Hernán Cortés landed at Veracruz in 1519 and began his conquest of the Aztec Empire, and Francisco Pizarro crossed the Andes to take on the Incas in 1532. Although the conquistadors didn't understand the causes of the epidemics that decimated native populations, they had a strong belief in their own prowess and in their divine mandate. Portugal explored Newfoundland and Labrador (which is actually named after Portuguese explorer João Fernandes Lavrador), as well as Brazil, where they gained a permanent foothold. In 1502, a Portuguese expedition arrived at the bay of Rio de Janiero. Among the crew in this expedition was a Florentine named Amerigo Vespucci, who published his bestseller *Mundus Novus* in 1504.

Given the prominence of Italians such as Columbus, Cabot, and Vespucci among the explorers, why were Spain and Portugal first to colonize the new world? It's true they had sea power; but they also had a license. In 1494, Spanish-born Pope Alexander VI presided over the Treaty of Tordesillas, which divided the western hemisphere between Spain and Portugal. The Pope split the globe at 47.37 west longitude and gave everything west of that line to the Spanish and everything east of it to the Portuguese. As long as Europe remained united under the Catholic Church, people obeyed the Papal edict. The Protestant Reformation began in the first decades of the 1500s, sparking a series of wars between Catholics and Protestants. But it wasn't until nearly a century later that Protestant European nations became strong and unified enough to look west. The defeat of the Armada in 1588 was a turning point for seagoing Protestants. As soon as they were able, the English and Dutch sent explorers. The Catholic French, who had been left out of the original Papal planetary division, took advantage of the lapse of the Roman decree and did the same.

The Treaty of Tordesillas divided the new world between Spain and Portugal, 1494.

Although it's safe to assume that fishermen had been landing for generations to dry their fish and replenish their drinking water for the trip home, the first successful permanent settlement on the North American coast was St. Augustine, established in 1585 in the Spanish colony of La Florida, followed by a French fort at Port Royal in what is now Nova Scotia, established in 1604. The English had tried settling people on Roanoke Island in 1588, but the colony had mysteriously disappeared by the time resupply ships returned to the area a few years later. The settlement may have been overrun by local Indians, but it's also possible that the abandoned colonists went to live with the natives when their food ran out and help failed to arrive from England. After losing their people and investment at Roanoke, the English tried again in 1607. The Virginia Company, a joint stock company chartered by King James I in 1606, sent two expeditions in 1607. One established Jamestown forty miles up the James River from Chesapeake Bay; the other established the unsuccessful Popham Colony on the Kennebec River in Maine.

Between the Virginia Company's two colonies, the Dutch established their first settlement at Fort Nassau in

Map depicting British attack on Spanish St. Augustine, 1586.

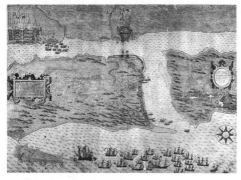

Captain John Smith's 1624 map of Virginia, featuring a large Indian warrior and Chief Powhatan in his longhouse.

1614, on the Hudson River near Albany, New York. Unlike England, Holland was also very active in South America, capturing a large portion of northern Brazil from the Portuguese and in 1600 conquering the Spanish city of Valdivia, on the Pacific coast in what is now southern Chile.

Holland and England also competed in the Caribbean. Because this region did not subsequently become part of the United States, it is often left out of American history books. As we'll see, this lapse is unfortunate. Trade with fellow Englishmen on islands such as Barbados, established in 1627, was a key to the survival of British colonies on the mainland.

Virginia

The coastline where the Chesapeake expedition of the Virginia Company first landed was already occupied. Indians lived in villages fortified with high palisade walls, so the English chose an unoccupied piece of swampy ground upriver that the Indians had shunned. Jamestown was plagued with mosquitos and other pests, but at least the natives didn't attack immediately. This was lucky, because the Virginia Company had sent a party consisting entirely of gentlemen. There were no farmers or tradesmen in the first settlement, since the had English expected to become rich trading with the natives. Even when they discovered there was no easy treasure to acquire, the Jamestown colonists still had no interest in farming. 82 of the original 120 colonists died in the first nine months.

The English were always acutely aware of the native presence, however. Indians are prominent on the 1624 map above, which labels the land upriver as Powhatan territory and includes an illustration of Chief Powhatan sitting in his long-house and a formidable-looking Indian warrior. Powhatan commanded an effective army, which his brother Opechancanough led in two wars against the English colony after the chief's death in 1618. Pocahontas, the chief's daughter whose marriage to Englishman John Rolfe had guarantee the peace between the Indians and English, had died of disease a year earlier in London.

New England

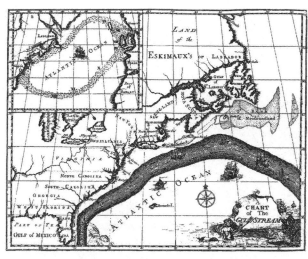

Although they had been aiming for the Carolinas, the Pilgrims arrived on Cape Cod in the winter of 1620. Our Thanksgiving traditions remember that the Pilgrims were unprepared for the severe weather they encountered, and nearly didn't make it through their first winter. But the stories don't always explain why. The New England coastline where the English, French, and Dutch landed was at the same latitude as Southern Spain, and the British colonies in Virginia were at the same latitudes as North Africa. Seventeenth-century Europeans were unaware that ocean currents were responsible for the temperate conditions they enjoyed on the northeastern edge of Europe. They mistakenly believed that latitude determined climate. This misconception hung on until the 1770s, when Benjamin Franklin's Chart of the Gulf Stream was first published in Europe. Note that Franklin includes the locations of George's Bank and the Grand Banks on his map. These fishing grounds remained of vital interest to both Americans and Europeans, and were actually mentioned in the treaties that concluded the Seven Years (French and Indian) War and the American Revolution.

The Puritans received a royal charter for a separate Massachusetts Bay Colony, and founded Boston in 1630. Between these two well-remembered dates, Peter Minuit established the Dutch colony of New Amsterdam in 1626 by purchasing Manhattan from Lenape natives who didn't

1660 view of New Amsterdam, which became New York in 1674.

own or even actually live on the island. According to tradition, Minuit paid the Lenape with a trunk of trade goods said to be worth 60 guilders, or $26 in modern money. While the facts of this story are probably true, calling this transaction a purchase ignores important cultural differences that affected the ways the parties understood the sale. Indian ideas of land ownership were much more fluid than those of the Europeans, and they probably perceived the trunk of goods as a symbolic gift rather than as a payment. This misunderstanding recurred frequently and led to land disputes throughout early American history.

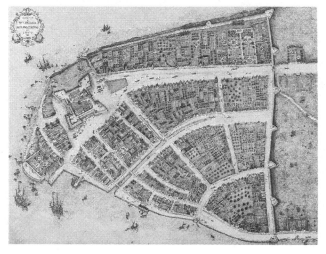

The Narragansett turkey (center) is a heritge breed developed in the 19th century by crossbreeding Black Spanish turkeys (left) reintroduced from Europe with wild turkeys of New England.

William Penn is similarly remembered as purchasing the land that became Pennsylvania from the people who lived there, although in fact he traced his ownership of a tract of land including the entire state of Pennsylvania and most of Delaware to a personal grant from King Charles II, in repayment of a debt the king owed Penn's father. The territory claimed by Holland was ceded to British control in 1674 and renamed New York after Charles II's younger brother, who was known as the Duke of York until he became King James II of England. In the 1660 map of the town on the previous page, a windmill is faintly visible just north of the battery. The city wall that became Wall Street is on the right.

One of the strange results of the long delay in North American settlement was that the English colonists brought back some New World plants and animals they didn't realize were actually from the Americas. When Scotch-Irish farmers were recruited to settle the New England frontier, they brought with them the seed potatoes that became a staple crop in Maine. Turkeys, carried to Europe by Columbus and bred in Spain, were reintroduced in the English colonies a century later and crossed with wild native birds, resulting in a range of heritage breeds leading to the commercial turkeys of today. Europeans also discovered valuable North American species such as the beaver, which became an important item of trade, especially in New France. Beaver felt was used to make hats for fashionable Europeans, and the beaver's habitat became an important element of territorial negotiations between the European nations claiming the New World.

Although they'd been delayed by events in Europe and began establishing serious colonies nearly a century after the Spanish and Portuguese, late arrival often worked to the North American colonists' advantage. In many cases, colonists found abandoned settlements, open fields waiting for their farmers, and park-like forests filled with game for their hunters. Disease, which had traveled much more quickly

1588 image of an Indian village, for a European book about Virginia.

through the densely populated south, had finally struck in the north. Native populations in the coastal northeast were devastated by an epidemic that raged from 1617 to 1619, killing 95 percent of the Abenaki people and over 90 percent of the Massachusetts tribe. This emptying of the land was seen by English settlers as a gift of divine providence. Puritan minister Cotton Mather wrote that "The Indians of these parts had newly...been visited with such a prodigious Pestilence; as carried away not a Tenth, but Nine Parts of Ten (yea, 'tis said Nineteen of Twenty) among them... So that the Woods were almost cleared of those pernicious Creatures, to make Room for better Growth" (*Magnalia Christi Americana*, 1702). English colonists had not deliberately wiped out the natives, but they were quick to take advantage of the open land and social chaos caused by the ongoing Columbian exchange.

Not only were populations decimated and cultures thrown into chaos, but political and military balances were upset throughout the area of European settlement. For example, Squanto, the good Indian of our Thanksgiving tradition, was a member of the Patuxet tribe who had been kidnapped as a child by an English captain and sold into slavery in Spain. Squanto escaped and after many years made his way back to his homeland, only to find that his entire village had been wiped out by disease and that a new English village, Plymouth, had been erected on its ruins. Squanto's family and all his allies were dead, leaving him without a home and

1585 painting by John White, Governor of the Roanoke Colony, shows an Indian village with cornfields.

without support against his village's traditional enemies. Squanto, who had learned to speak English while a slave in Europe, allied himself with the Pilgrims and helped them survive their first winter partly because he had nowhere else to go. We shouldn't underestimate the social chaos caused by the deaths of more than nine out of ten people in the native world, especially when we're trying to understand why Indians reacted as they did to European colonists.

Land Management

Native Americans had lived in the areas Europeans colonized for about 11,000 years, since the glacier covering New England and the Great Lakes had retreated at the end of the last ice age. The natives had techniques and traditions that

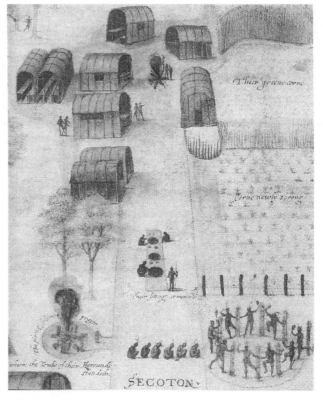

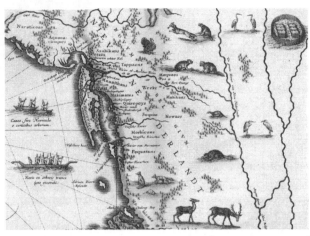

Detail from a 1635 Dutch map showing wildlife wealth and Indian fortifications. North is to the right.

some Europeans studied closely. But for many settlers, Indian practices seemed strange and uncivilized. One reason Europeans misunderstood Native culture was that it was very different from European culture, especially in the way the Americans used the land and its resources. Unlike the urban empires the Spanish had found in Central and South America, many North American Indians lived in small, mobile communities. In what became the mid-Atlantic colonies and southern New England, natives didn't build cities. They moved with the seasons, from winter hunting grounds where they lived in single-family wigwams to summer farmlands where they occupied communal long-houses. In the spring, when fish species like shad and alewife were running upstream to their spawning grounds, coastal natives congregated around streams and rivers. From October to March, Indian men went into the deep forest to hunt beaver, caribou, moose, deer, and bear. The natives had no livestock, since most of the large mammals of North America had disappeared in the Holocene Extinction, leaving no species susceptible to domestication. So women gardened while men hunted and fished.

The crops Native American women cultivated are called the three sisters. Maize was planted in hills rather than rows. Beans planted around the maize plants climbed the cornstalks and their roots converted nitrogen from the air, enriching the soil. Squash or pumpkins planted between the hills shaded the soil and held back weeds. These intensively gardened plots were called tangles, and they produced remarkably high yields per acre. After a year or two of gardening in one location, native women would shift their plantings to another field, allowing soil fertility to recover naturally.

Indian women planted the three sisters, as memorialized on US $1 coin.

In the forests, North American natives regularly burned the understory to encourage new growth. Fire created what ecologists call the edge effect, attracting game animals and boosting their numbers by providing abundant food. The hunters' paradise Europeans wrote so frequently about in promotional tracts to lure investors and settlers to the new world was neither a providential accident nor a natural feature of the land. It was the result of deliberate native land and game management. But because most European settlers didn't understand the ecology of their new home or native practices, they got the impression Indian men were lazy and expected their women to support them.

It has long been known that Indians used fire to clear land and to burn the understory of the forest. But historians have only recently begun to appreciate the extent of Indian burning. Great expanses of the eastern seaboard were cleared for farming by annual burns. Fire kept forests open and encouraged growth of foods preferred by wildlife, creating the park-like woodlands so admired by Europeans. Indian burning continued for centuries, until eastern forests became full of fire-loving tree species like slash pine, whose cones only open and release seeds when exposed to flames. Scientists have recently suggested that the Little Ice Age, which reached its coldest temperatures in the sixteenth and seventeenth centuries, may have been exacerbated by the destruction of the Indian cultures that burned the Americas. The end of burning and the rapid regrowth of American forests removed so much carbon from the atmosphere that scientists now believe the elimination of the Indians caused by the Columbian exchange may have helped trigger global cooling.

Misconceptions

Native Americans' mobile culture and land use traditions were so different from the lifestyles the settlers had known in Europe, that many colonists failed to notice that the natives knew what they were doing until it was too late. By the early 1800s, coastal Indians had mostly disappeared and forests had reverted to their natural state. Descendants of the English settlers lamented that turkeys, deer, and other animals that had provided so much free meat for their ancestors were gone from the woods. The English hadn't hunted these species to extinction. There were just no Indians managing the land to provide the high levels of food the wildlife had depended on. In a famous account of his travels through New England, Yale president Timothy Dwight remarked, "Hunting with us exists chiefly in the tales of other times."

Some species such as the passenger pigeon were actually hunted to extinction, but the story of the passenger pigeon is more complicated than that description might suggest. Native to the northeastern region of the continent, pigeon populations had exploded when there were no longer Indians managing the land, until the birds lived in flocks of several million. Passenger pigeons took advantage of the abundant food

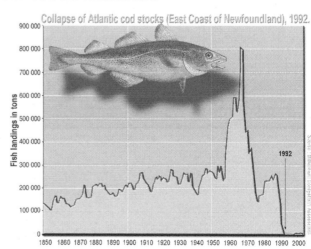

Collapse of Atlantic cod stocks (East Coast of Newfoundland), 1992.

1909 schoolbook image of Peter Minuit's purchase of Manhattan reflects Euro-American concepts of ownership and sale.

sources produced by Indian land management, once the Indians were no longer present to protect and use the landscapes they had created. One flock, seen flying in the mid-nineteenth century in southern Ontario, was a mile wide and three hundred miles long. The pigeons took fourteen hours to pass the people observing them. Passenger pigeons were shot and trapped throughout the seventeenth, eighteenth and nineteenth centuries, and as cities grew their habitats shrank. The last passenger pigeon, named Martha, died on September 1st, 1914.

The offshore cod fisheries, which had supported countless generations of Native Americans and Europeans, were also harvested to near extinction. Cod had dependably provided hundreds of tons of food each year for centuries, until severe overfishing at the end of the twentieth century caused a population collapse the species has not yet recovered from, and perhaps never will.

Another of our misconceptions about Native Americans is that they had no concept of ownership. This is the reverse of the idea that Indians shared European concepts of property and payment, which was used to justify the purchase of Manhattan and countless other parcels of Indian land. Both ideas are based on a mistaken attempt to fit Indian concepts into a format that makes sense to us, and both are inaccurate. Native cultures developed in response to their experiences in the Americas. So Indians had different traditions about common use and private ownership, and their ideas about land use represented a relationship with the environment that Europeans misunderstood. When native people sold a parcel of land to Europeans, for example, the earliest contracts and deeds usually specified that the sellers retained their rights to hunt and fish on the land, and even sometimes to set up temporary settlements as they moved across the region from season to season. Later, as the balance of power shifted, the language of land contracts changed to reflect European ideas of ownership. As the European population grew, even where earlier contracts had preserved their use rights, Indians were often prevented from exercising them. Natives also had a different concept of money and its role in social relations. Living in a mobile culture that valued reciprocity, Indians used wampum and trade goods not as mediums of exchange or symbols of wealth, but as ceremonial gifts to be given at feasts and gatherings to demonstrate and celebrate social relationships.

Although many individual settlers probably tried to deal fairly with their American neighbors, the difference between European and na-

1772 engraving of Metacomet, by Paul Revere.

tive ideas of ownership and the rapid growth of the colonies made conflict virtually inevitable. Natives moved to new locations as the seasons changed. They gardened in shifting fields. Colonists built houses and permanent villages, and fenced their fields. But although they claimed complete ownership of the parcels they occupied, the colonists let their cattle and pigs run loose over the countryside. When Indians treated European livestock like wildlife and shot a wandering cow, or when they killed pigs eating their unfenced crops, the colonists demanded compensation for the destruction of their property. And of course, more colonists arrived every year. The Powhatan wars in Virginia (1610-46), the Pequot War in Connecticut (1637), the Dutch-Indian War in the Hudson Valley (1643), and the Beaver Wars (1650) all ended badly for the natives. Even King Philip's War (1675), which is remembered as a nearly-successful uprising by Massasoit's son, Metacomet, who had finally decided enough was enough, resulted in five times as many native deaths as European. By the conclusion of the French and Indian War (1756-63), northeastern natives were no longer a threat to European colonies.

Commerce

Although our histories traditionally portray the North American colonies as havens for freedom-seeking religious dissenters like the Pilgrims, Puritans, and Quakers, it's important to remember that the European interest in the Americas was always commercial. South American gold and silver enriched the treasuries of Spain and its trade partners. Caribbean sugar plantations were established by Portuguese and Dutch entrepreneurs and later taken over by Englishmen. American commodities like tobacco, beaver pelts, and cod made merchants and investors rich on both sides of

Histories focused on North America often forget the importance of the Caribbean to the survival and growth of the continental colonies.

the Atlantic. Boosters of American colonization and investment insisted that the new world was filled with natural wealth just waiting to be exploited. And if a resource was scarce in Europe, that just added to its value in America. American wildlife, and even trees, were highly valued by crowded European nations that had long ago cut down most of their own forests and killed most of their game. The British Navy had all the tall pines of northern New England marked with the King's arrow because there were no trees in Europe tall enough to make masts. It was ille-

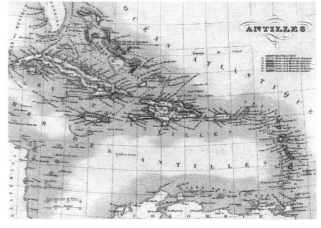

African slaves process-ing tobacco on a Virginia plantation, 1670.

gal to cut the King's trees, and according to New England folklore, there are still some old trees deep in the Maine woods with the King's mark on them.

American colonists' expectations for the new world included not only a place to build a new society, but a place where they could get rich. Even religious idealists like the Pilgrims looked forward to opportunities for social mobility that were unavailable to them in England. And right from the start, European colonies in North America were commercial. In addition to fishing, growing tobacco, and trapping beaver, the North American colonies benefited from the booming sugar economy of the Caribbean. Islands such as Barbados that had once been self-sufficient had begun by the mid-1600s to specialize in the highly profitable commodity, so they looked to their neighbor colonies for food supplies. John Winthrop, the Puritan leader who helped establish Boston and who was Governor of the Massachusetts Bay Colony four times before 1650, sent his second son Henry to help establish Barbados in 1626. When Oliver Cromwell's English Civil War stopped the flow of commerce to the ten-year-old Bay Colony in 1640, trade with the West Indies saved Boston's economy. Governor Winthrop's younger son Samuel joined the growing community of New England merchants in the Caribbean sugar islands in 1647.

In the South, cultivation of the Virginia colony's main cash crop tobacco for the European market required lots of cheap labor. At first, many of the workers were poor English men and women, who came to the colonies as indentured servants. Later, when the supply of British workers was cut off by the English Civil War, and then by the American Revolution, Southern planters began to rely on enslaved Africans, who were already being used on West Indies sugar plantations, to do the work.

Europeans settling in North America not only brought ideas about the environment developed in their home countries, they brought a commitment to commodity export markets that helped shape their social and political structures and their ideas about the land they found. The North American landscapes that became the colonies had been carefully managed for centuries by the Indians living on them. The disappearance of the Indians and establishment of the colonies rearranged these landscapes in the image of the old world. Traditions and practices that had sustained native populations for thousands of years were lost when disease and war destroyed Indian cultures. It's interesting to speculate whether those practices would have been abandoned anyway, because the natives' mobile lifestyle was incompatible with the commerce and growth the rapidly expanding colonies needed. Or whether colonists encountering a more active, ongoing display of Indian land management might have made different choices for the American landscape.

Further Reading

Colin G. Calloway, *New Worlds for All: Indians, Europeans, and the Remaking of Early America.* 2013.

William Cronon, *Changes in the Land: Indians, Colonists, and the Ecology of New England.* 1983.

Matthew Parker, *The Sugar Barons: Family, Corruption, Empire, and War in the West Indies.* 2012.

Supplement: Changing How We See the Land

William Cronon's 1983 history of early New England, *Changes in the Land*, is often the first Environmental History book college students read. The book has also done fairly well with the general public, introducing popular audiences to some of Environmental History's themes while telling an engaging story that challenges long-held beliefs about English Colonists and Indians.

Cronon's story of early New England builds on the idea that colonists' attraction to New England was a response to the abundance they discovered, influenced by the scarcity they had experienced back home. English colonists, Cronon said, were part of a transatlantic market economy and drew the Indians into this economy as well. The pre-colonial landscape Cronon presented was quite different from the trackless wilderness described in traditional histories, and his detailed descriptions of the landscape and the ways Indians lived on it are among the most attractive features of the book.

Cronon observed that "Many European visitors were struck by what seemed to them the poverty of Indians who lived in the midst of a landscape endowed so astonishingly with abundance." But English prejudices against the natives were based on a misunderstanding of the Indian approach to life and land use. Natives didn't live in large houses surrounded by lots of possessions, so Europeans assumed they were poor. Cronon said the Indians were actually managing their environment in sophisticated ways that the colonists completely failed to recognize. Burning the forest understory created edge environments preferred by game animals. Gardening in tangles of maize, beans, and squash maximized crop yields, reduced erosion, and increased soil fertility; especially relative to the colonists' monoculture of wheat. Keeping their population density low made the Indians' lifestyle sustainable.

Cronon's point was that the Indians had a more stable, sustainable approach to their environment than the colonists. But the Indian lifestyle required mobility, which made it incompatible with settled European agriculture. Cronon contrasted the Indians' seasonal migrations with the colonists' construction of fences. He borrowed a bit from ecology, invoking Liebig's Law to explain low Indian population densities, saying "biological populations are limited not by the total annual resources available to them but by the minimum amount that can be found at the scarcest time of year." Unaware of how the Indians had actively shaped their environment, English colonists who had been restricted from hunting by Game Laws in their home country over-hunted and let the woods grow wild. The wildlife disappeared along with the Indians.

Chapter Four: Frontier and Grid

In this chapter we explore the lure of the Western Frontier on colonists and early Americans, and how people began expanding westward from the initial European settlements in North America.

Looking at Colonial North America, we noticed that many early English coastal settlements were established on sites previously used by natives. As settlement moved westward, European Americans were less likely to be able to take advantage of native improvements. As time passed, the fields and forests Indians had cleared filled in again. And sometimes settlers farther west found Indians still occupying their ancestral lands and unwilling to share. Many settlers tried to choose uncontested places to make their homes. They were not always successful, as the long string of nineteenth-century Indian Wars shows.

The continent was large and the population density of native cultures was often much lower than that of the Europeans. Though there were always pioneers willing to take their chances in Indian Country, most settler families moved to regions already considered U.S. Territory. Although there were some notable exceptions, most of these regions were reasonably safe from Indians, who had already been pushed farther west. So for most settlers the idea of moving west involved less fighting Indians and more clearing unoccupied land to make it productive for their new

Boundary between Mississippi River and
49th parallel uncertain due to misconception that
source of Mississippi River lay further north   1775

George Washington's 1753 map of the beginning of the Ohio River, at present-day Pittsburgh.

style of European-influenced American agriculture.

The frontier has always been a powerful magnet for the American imagination. It's not well remembered in most of our histories, but one of the grievances that led to the American Revolution was colonial anger that the British had accommodated their Indian allies after the Seven Years War (1756-63) by limiting the colonies' westward expansion. The Cherokee Nation and the powerful Haudenosaunee (Iroquois Confederacy) had sided with the British against the French and other native nations. But like the other natives, England's Indian allies were alarmed by the inexorable growth of the colonies and wanted some assurance that their territories would be respected. In 1751, Benjamin Franklin had boasted that for every baby born in Britain, two were born in America and soon there would be more Englishmen in the New World than in the old. The Iroquois, whose homelands included what is now western New York and Pennsylvania, saw their way of life threatened by expanding English settlement. So, as a reward for the Indians' support and out of respect for the Confederacy's military strength, the British government issued a proclamation establishing a western colonial boundary. The Proclamation Line followed the Appalachian Mountains, cutting through western New York and Pennsylvania and creating an Indian Reserve stretching from the Great Lakes to the Gulf of Mexico.

The British colonists were enraged. Many of their royal charters had given the colonies land grants extending to the Pacific Ocean. The Crown's acknowledgement of Indian claims to that territory was a betrayal of their futures, the colonists claimed. And for many, the issue was more than symbolic. Following the proclamation, wealthy land speculators like George Washington instructed their agents to buy as much Indian land west of the mountains as possible, but Washington warned his partners to keep "this whole matter a profound secret." A lot of the surveying work Washington was famous for doing as a young man, he did on the wrong side of the Proclamation Line.

When the Sons of Liberty and the Continental Congress met in Philadelphia and drafted the Declaration of Independence, one of their complaints against King George III was that he had unleashed "merciless Indian savages" against the colonists. Indians continued to resist when colonists appeared on their lands. Many Indians sided with Britain during the Revolution, seeing British control of the Americas as their best hope of retaining their land and sovereignty. Unfortunately for the natives, the colonists won their independence. At the Treaty of Paris in 1783, Britain signed its claim to all the territory east of the Mississippi over to the United States. Although the new nation's economic fate depended heavily on its being part of an Atlantic trading community, the unconquered frontier to the west was a strong influence on American policy and culture.

When the United States took its first census in 1790, Americans discovered that half their population was under the age of 16. At the end of the eighteenth century, the American birthrate was higher than any birthrate ever recorded in a European nation. For comparison, it was more than double the highest birthrate achieved during the post-World War II, 1950s baby boom.

America's growing population needed an outlet. To take a representative example, the western Massachusetts hill-town Ashfield, where I've done a lot of research, contained 130 families in the early 1800s. Most of the residents were farmers; even the town doctor kept a cow and raised hay to feed it and his horses. The average family had five children. The town's largest families had eleven.

As the children of Ashfield and other young Americans grew up, they naturally looked west. In contrast with the colonial Hudson Valley, which had developed a feudal social structure of large estates and tenant farmers, and the tidewater South, which had developed an economy dominated by plantations worked by slaves, New England and the Middle Colonies had established a system of small-scale land ownership that continued after independence, creating large numbers of modest, self-sufficient farms. Yeoman farmers owned their land and fed their families and livestock from its produce. If they had surpluses they would sell them, often to the town miller who would aggregate local products and sell them in Eastern cities. Some farmers even grew specialty crops (Ashfield happened to specialize in peppermint). But their focus, if push came to shove, was feeding their families. And as those families grew, feeding everyone became harder to do.

Most farm families owned about 80 acres, and in a town like Ashfield much of that land was wooded hills and rocky pastures, impossible to cultivate. While a hard-working farm

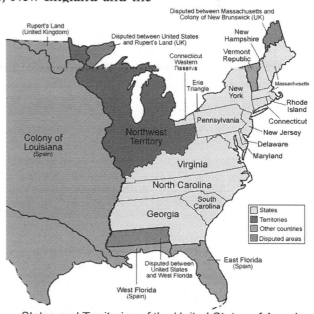

States and Territories of the United States of America
August 7 1789 to April 2 1790

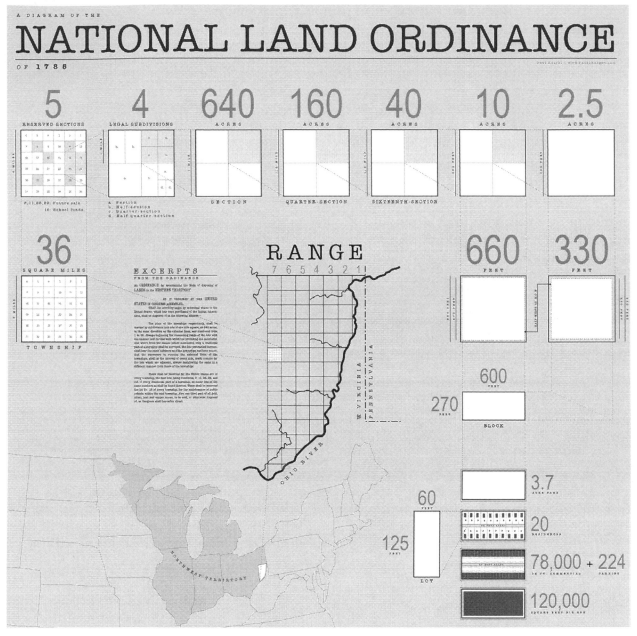

family could feed itself, only one son could inherit the farm and have enough tillable land to support a new family. The rest of the children had to repeat the work of their parents and start a new farm.

The new United States government made it easy for young families to start new farms. Congress appointed a committee that included Thomas Jefferson, to figure out how to dispose of the land the nation had acquired in the 1783 Peace Treaty with England. Technically this territory belonged to the nation rather than to the thirteen states, and since under the Articles of Confederation, Congress was not allowed to levy taxes, land sales were seen as an appropriate way to raise funds to run the government. The result was The Northwest Ordinance, which created the Northwest Territory and specified the way western lands would be surveyed, parceled, and sold. The Ordinance decreed that townships would be six-mile squares divided into thirty-six lots, called sections, of one square mile each. Five of these sections would be reserved for government or public purposes, including lot number sixteen in the center of each township, which would hold a mandatory public school. With half the nation's population under age sixteen, free public education was considered a key to American progress, so it was built into one of our earliest national laws.

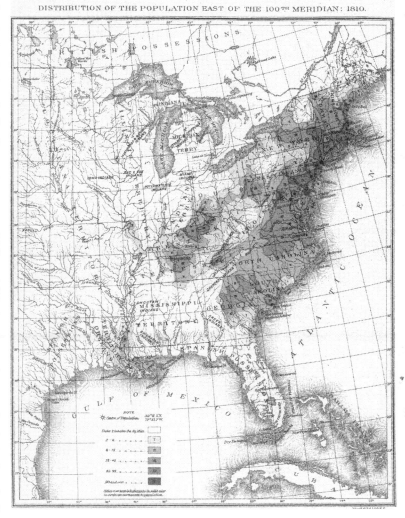

DISTRIBUTION OF THE POPULATION EAST OF THE 100TH MERIDIAN: 1810.

Each square-mile section contained 640 acres of land, which could be subdivided into quarter-sections of 160 acres each or half-quarter sections of 80 acres, which most people considered the smallest size for a successful farm. In towns and cities, land could be subdivided down to 60 by 125 foot single family building lots. The price of the land on the frontier would remain low for most of the nineteenth century, beginning at $1 per acre and later rising to $1.25. In the cities, speculation could quickly drive land prices up, causing property bubbles like the one that inflated Chicago real estate values by 40,000 percent in the early 1830s, driving land prices to New York City levels before bursting in a storm of foreclosures in 1841.

Western New York and the territory just west of the Ohio River were among the first public lands to be surveyed and sold. Ashfield families like the Ranneys (whose family letters you'll read in the chapter supplement) followed the Mohawk Valley and made farms in territory taken during the Revolutionary War from the Haudenosaunee. Like many forward-looking families, the Ranneys invested in frontier land in Michigan at the same time they were moving from Massachusetts to New York.

Just a few years after the family moved west, several of the younger Ranney brothers moved farther west. But family ties held, and the Ranneys stayed in close contact throughout their lives.

Settlers from Connecticut and New Jersey rushed into the Ohio River Valley, which was close to Virginia and Western Pennsylvania across the old Proclamation Line. Ohio Valley land was prized because although it was difficult bringing wagon-loads of farm products across the Allegheny Mountains to market, the Ohio River began at Fort Pitt (Pittsburgh) and flowed into the Mississippi at what is now the southern tip of Illinois. Enterprising farmers could float their surplus grain down the rivers to the Spanish port of New Orleans, where merchants could put it on ships bound for East Coast Cities, the Caribbean, or even Europe.

Western New York filled quickly. Settlement of the Ohio Valley was equally rapid, and the Ohio Territory became a state in 1803. Many new Ohio farmers were from the middle states like Connecticut and New Jersey, whose original colonial charters had included parts of the Northwest Territory. As they left their settled homelands and cut new farms out of wild land, these Yankee farmers started a pattern that would repeat itself many times over the next century.

This illustration from a French account of travel in America in 1796 is pretty accurate. The fields are full of tree stumps and the pioneer wife is standing about as far as she ever got from the smoky hearth.

An American Log-house.

Pioneer Farmers

The image above was the sight that awaited many settler families, when they arrived at the parcel they had often bought sight unseen from the land office. Their new homestead was often trackless forest. Old growth woodlands covered most of the area between the Atlantic coast and the Mississippi, so this experience was repeated again and again. Before doing anything else, settlers moving to western Massachusetts in the 1760s, or western New York in the 1810s, or Michigan in the 1830s would need to build a shelter and clear enough land to raise the crops that would get them through the first winter and feed a few animals. Settlers often cleared fields by girdling trees, cutting a broad strip of bark to kill the tree. They planted corn Indian-style in hills between the standing deadwood. The following season, they cut and burned the dead trees, and after rotting a few years the stumps could be removed and the field plowed for wheat. A hardworking settler family could clear about 7 acres per year. The ashes from the burned forest provided nutrients for the soil and also potash for sale in the eastern cities. Potash was used to make soap, and was often the first product western settlers shipped back to eastern merchants.

Pioneer life was very hard work. In addition to clearing land, pasturing animals, and raising crops, settlers had to cut and split from thirty to forty cords of firewood per year for heating and cooking. Women spent much of their time cooking, which is a slow and tiring process when you do it over an open fire in a one-room cabin. In their spare time pioneer women raised their five children and wove cloth to make the family's clothing.

After a couple of decades, a successful settler family usually had 20 to 30 acres of improved land and a substantial woodlot to supply their annual firewood needs. Since the frontier had been surveyed into townships on the grid, there was usually a village or town within walking distance, providing a school, social life and a small market for surplus goods. Merchants often took produce from farmers in payment for manufactured goods and supplies the farmers could not make themselves. The merchant shipped farm products to cities for consumption or export, and bought a supply of city goods once or twice a year to sell in town. By the time the farm was well established the family was usually quite large. One son, usually the youngest, would inherit the farm in return for taking care of his parents at the ends of their lives. The older sons, who would be adults long before their parents were ready to give up working, often moved farther west.

Col. John Wayles Jefferson, grandson of Thomas Jefferson and his slave Sally Hemings, fought in the Civil War on the Union side.

Free Soil

The Northwest Ordinance, which was passed in 1787 before the Constitution was even ratified, opened the territory that

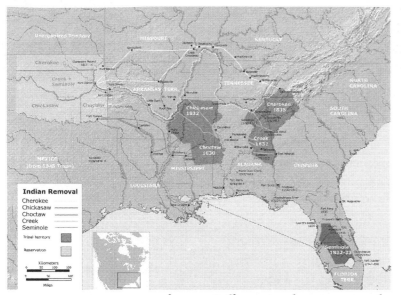

would become Ohio, Indiana, Illinois, Michigan, Wisconsin, and Minnesota. In addition to establishing the grid and setting aside land for public schools, one of the most important elements of the Ordinance was that it prohibited slavery in the territories. This prohibition had a major impact on the environment because it prevented the spread of large plantations and encouraged the style of land ownership and family farming we now associate with Thomas Jefferson's ideal of the independent yeoman farmer. Jefferson, a slave-owner who wrote eloquently about freedom and equality, was a living symbol of the young nation's moral struggle. Many northern farmers moving west came from old Yankee families with long traditions of abolitionism. Others understood that their small-farm produce would have trouble competing in the market with farm products made using the unpaid labor of plantation slaves. Many western farmers joined Free Soil political groups that helped create the anti-slavery Republican Party and elect Abraham Lincoln. Thomas Jefferson's 1803 Louisiana Purchase doubled the size of the United States and opened an even wider territory for expansion, extending all the way to what is now the Idaho border in the northwest. But ironically, it also reopened the conflict over slavery in the territories.

Trail of Tears

By 1810, after nearly a generation of westward expansion, the Ohio and Cumberland River Valleys were beginning to look like the settled areas back east. Cincinnati, Frankfort, and Nashville were becoming centers of commerce, as was Buffalo New York on the shore of Lake Erie. Saint Louis on the Mississippi and Detroit on the western end of Lake Erie were also growing, as people continued looking to the frontier for new opportunities. In the Southern States, westward expansion of the plantation system was challenged by the Cherokee, Creek, Choctaw, Chickasaw, and Seminole nations. The Indians had adopted many of the elements of Euro-American culture, including a two-house legislature, a legal system based on that of the United States, and even slavery. But Southern planters lobbied the government to remove the Indians and make western lands available for their own expansion. The Indian Removal Act of 1830 was actually judged unconstitutional by an 1832 Supreme Court decision (Worcester v. Georgia) that ruled in favor of the natives. But President Andrew Jackson ignored the court's decision and the natives were removed to the Indian Territory that later became Oklahoma, along the infamous Trail of Tears.

The Erie Canal at Lockport, New York, 1839.

Transport & Commerce

Along with population pressure, one of the main factors accelerating western settlement was improving transportation technology. Although they were far from eastern cities and understood the need to remain self-sufficient, many westerner settlers still considered themselves part of the Atlantic commercial world. Success beyond mere subsistence for a growing number of farmers depended on their ability to get their produce to eastern markets. The first phases of expansion had allowed farmers to use rivers like the Hudson in New York and the Allegheny and Ohio in the Middle West, to float their surpluses to markets like New York City, St. Louis, and New Orleans. The growth of trade convinced Americans that transportation was the key to expanding the frontier. We'll return to this topic in greater detail in Chapter Six, but here's an early example. The Erie Canal, begun in 1817 and completed in 1825, opened not only western New York, but the entire Great Lakes region to commercial shipping. Less than ten years after the canal opened, the last fulling mills that

Note the six-by-six mile square townships and numbered sections still shown on this 20th-century map.

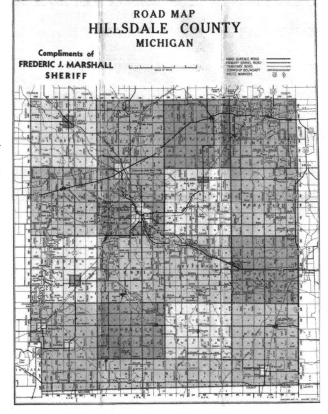

DISTRIBUTION OF THE POPULATION EAST OF THE 100TH MERIDIAN: 1850.

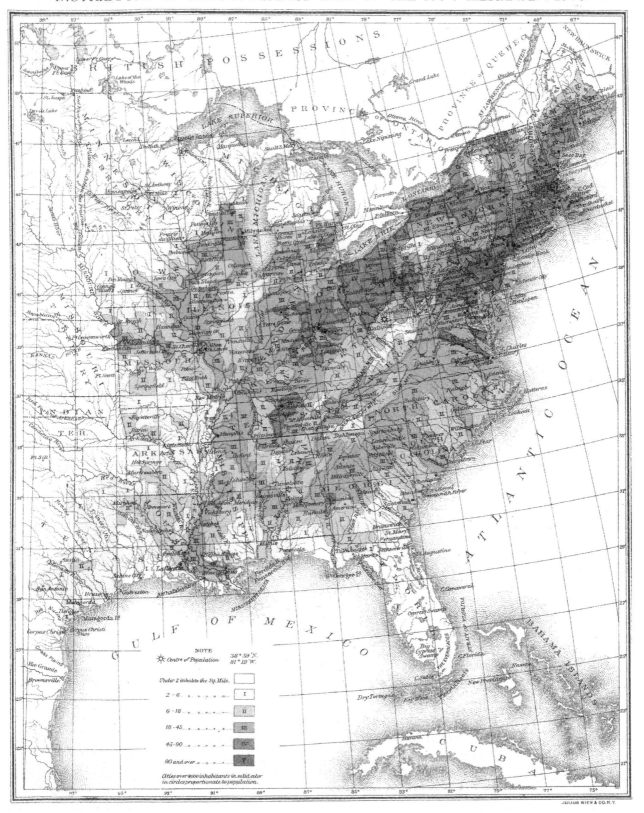

processed homespun cloth disappeared from the Mohawk Valley, as farm wives jumped at the opportunity to reduce their workload by buying eastern textiles.

By 1830, after nearly another generation of growth, the sons of farmers who had moved to the Ohio Valley and Western New York were on the move again. This time, their destinations were Illinois, Indiana and Southern Michigan. Cincinnati and Louisville were now major cities, and settlement was extending up the Missouri as well as the Mississippi River. The federal government sold most of the land between the original 13 states and the Mississippi during the first half of the 19th century. Beginning with the Northwest Territory, the land was surveyed and the township grid laid out. This pattern of settlement can still be seen in satellite images, or even from the windows of planes when you fly over the Midwest. The average size of a working farm today is closer to a full mile-square section than the quarter or half-quarter section settlers had bought at the land office, but the grid pattern can still be seen from the air. Farm technology like John Deere's 1838 steel plow and Cyrus McCormick's reaper, patented in 1837, helped western farms produce wheat for the commercial market. Bad harvests in Great Britain and wars in Europe provided high profits to exporters. More eastern farmers moved west, often selling their old farms at profits that allowed them to buy substantially more land at cheaper western rates. The government Land Office's typical price in the first half of the nineteenth century remained $1.25 per acre.

By the middle of the nineteenth century, Midwestern farmers were solidly embedded in an international commercial network. Cincinnati, on the Ohio River was packing so much bacon and salt pork that the city became known as Porkopolis. The end of Europe's Crimean War in 1856 cut grain prices by two thirds, helping to trigger the Panic of 1857 and a recession that lasted several years. Like it or not, American farmers settling the frontier were a key element of America's growing power in international commerce.

Family Ties

Historians and novelists have often claimed that pioneers moving West severed all their ties with homes and families, suggesting that migration to the frontier may have helped produce the individualism and focus on nuclear families considered such a distinctive part of the American character. It's quite true that it took courage and self-reliance to settle the Midwest or to travel all the way to the west coast, which before the completion of the transcontinental railroad in 1869 required a grueling trip on foot or horseback across the continent or a dangerous ocean voyage around the Straits of Magellan at the bottom of South America. But remarkably, families managed to stay connected in spite of these distances. For example, the Ranneys, whose letters to each other you'll read in the chapter supplement, were a Scotch-Irish family who had arrived in Colonial Connecticut in the 17th century. Several brothers moved to Ashfield Massachusetts about 1790, and several of their sons moved on to Phelps in western New York in the 1830s. A few years later, several of the Ranney brothers and cousins moved on to Michigan. Oldest brother, Alonso Franklin Ranney (portrait on previous page), made Phelps his lifelong home. A couple of brothers went even further and had adventures in the Indian Territory and the California Gold Rush. But throughout the nineteenth century, the brothers kept in touch by letter, visited each other, and even did regular business with each other. Michigan Ranneys sold farm produce to their merchant brother Henry in Massachusetts. Many American pioneers considered themselves part of extended families and held onto family connections in spite of great distance and limited communications.

Immigration

Bridget O'Donnell and her children, from an 1849 newspaper.

Immigrants from Britain and Europe joined the westward flow of farmers and farmers' sons. America's poor diplomatic relations with England hampered immigration until after the War of 1812, but the war's resolution opened the floodgates. Continuing wars in Europe and the social upheavals of the industrial revolution created a flow of immigration that continued throughout the nineteenth century. In the late 1840s, nearly half the immigrants were Irish, fleeing the agricultural disaster known as the Irish Potato famine. Unlike the Andean Indians who had developed hundreds of varieties of potatoes for a wide range of purposes, Europeans grew only a few varieties bred from imported seed potatoes. Most of the two million acres of potatoes in Ireland were a single variety, the Irish Lumper.

Potatoes were so cheap to grow, reliable, and high-yielding that the population in Ireland had exploded by the early nineteenth century. From a starting point around one and a half million in 1600, Ireland's population grew by 600 percent in 200 years, reaching about nine million people by the early 1800s. Of those nine million people, four out of ten (or over three and a half million) ate no solid food but potatoes.

The first reports of potato blight in Ireland came in September, 1845. In the next two months, the blight wiped out about three quarters of a million acres of potatoes. The next year was worse. And the year after that. Over a million people died, and about a million and a half fled Ireland. By 1850, Irish immigrants made up over half the populations of Boston, New York, Baltimore, and Philadelphia.

After 1850, immigration from Germany accelerated as Germans fled the chaos caused by their revolutions of 1848 and 1849. Over 42 million Americans of German descent were counted in the 2000 census, making German-Americans the largest ethnic group in America. While some of these German and Irish immigrants farmed, many became tradesmen, factory workers and laborers in Northeastern cities and in the newer cities of the northern frontier. Pittsburgh, Toledo, Milwaukee, Chicago, and Bismarck North Dakota were all listed in the 1900 census as having populations of between 50 and 75 percent "whites of foreign parentage." The black population, of course, was still largely trapped by slavery and its aftermath in the South. The slave economy is also cited as a major cause of low immigration to Southern states in the 19th century, since farmers or wage-workers from Europe had no place in a society where all the work was done by plantation slaves and later by destitute share-croppers.

No Decline

For a long time, historians believed that at about the same time the Civil War destroyed the plantation system in the South, transportation and western farms killed agriculture in the old northeast. This belief influenced the Country Life policies of Progressives in the early 20th century and has lived on in current farm and environmental policy, as we'll see in later chapters. But if we look closer at the details, a different picture emerges. New England farmlands continued increasing and forests continued shrinking until the last few years of the 19th century, when New England was over 90% deforested. This was long after the Midwest had taken over as the breadbasket of staple crops like wheat and corn. Hillside Yankee farm fields where it had been difficult to grow wheat became pastures for Merino Sheep, which became

Both Eastern and Western farms actually thrived throughout the nineteenth century.

RES. OF L. F. SHEARER, ENFIELD, MASS.

a highly sought-after premium breed. Growing cities certainly lured people off eastern farms to work in factories like the textile mills of the Merrimack Valley which we'll cover in Chapter Five, but urban growth also provided a lucrative market for farm products. And although easterners with their small, hillside fields could no longer keep pace with the Midwestern farmer in corn or wheat production, they could easily outcompete him on milk and hay. The bulkier and more perishable a product was, the greater the advantage for the local farmer. Eastern farmers became dairymen and grew hay to feed urban horses (before the age of cars and trucks, there were a lot of urban horses). Eastern truck farms grew fruits and perishable vegetables for nearby city people. As cities grew, there were more and more factory and office workers who earned wages rather than producing their own food. This division of labor created a new profession and a special class of people, American farmers, who were responsible for feeding the rest of us. This major shift in American culture also had major implications for the environment, as we'll see.

It's easy looking back from the present, when few Americans can claim to be self-sufficient, to romanticize the Yeoman farmer or the pioneer. Many historians share this romantic perspective, and some even insist that nineteenth century farmers fled westward to avoid the degrading capitalism of the cities. However, except for a small number who joined religious settlements or utopian communes, most of the settlers who moved west remained interested in the culture and commerce of the eastern cities. Like the Mohawk Valley farm wives who abandoned home weaving as soon as the Erie Canal brought affordable eastern textiles, most Americans who moved west tried to maintain a healthy balance between commerce and self-sufficiency. The terms of the negotiation have changed over time, but the challenge to find that balance is one we still face today.

Further Reading

Christopher Clark, *The Roots of Rural Capitalism*. 1990.

Susan E. Gray, *The Yankee West: Community Life on the Michigan Frontier*. 1996.

Malcolm Rohrbough, *The Land Office Business: The Settlement and Administration of American Public Lands, 1789-1837*, 1968. *The Trans-Appalachian Frontier*, 2008.

Supplement:
Seeing with the eyes of the past

Primary sources are documents written by actual people who lived in the past. Town historical societies are great places to find them. As I was doing research toward my dissertation in Ashfield Massachusetts, I came across a series of family letters written by six out of a set of eight brothers (they had one sister whose letters didn't make it into this archive). The Ranney brothers were all born between 1812 and 1833 in Ashfield, and all of them but third son Henry went west—some farther than others. They wrote each other regularly for more than fifty years, and over a hundred of their letters are preserved at the Ashfield Historical Society. Because the writers were all brothers, little time is wasted on empty formality. They get right to the point and write about what's most important to the family. The letters offer a rare glimpse at the interests and concerns of a normal American family as they experienced life in the nineteenth century.

Henry S. Ranney, 1817-1899.

Letter #1

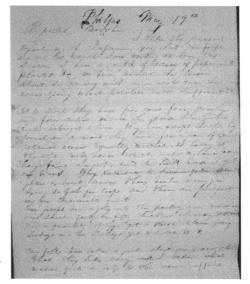

The story begins in May, 1839, with a three-page letter from twenty-four year-old Lewis Ranney to his younger brother Henry. Lewis begins with the most important news: "our folks are well as usual." Their parents, George and Achsah, had moved most of the family to Phelps New York in 1833. Henry, sixteen at the time, was working as a clerk for an Ashfield merchant and stayed behind. Lewis was living at home in 1839 when he wrote to Henry—but he had already decided he was moving on to Michigan.

The contents of the letter reveal the topics Lewis knew his brother would want to hear about. First, news of both the immediate and extended family. Then, apparently in response to a request in Henry's letter, Lewis lists the birth dates of all the siblings. Their mother, Achsah Ranney, had eleven children in the 21-year period between age 23 and 44, and then lived to 80. Nine of these children had survived childhood and were alive in 1839. Lewis tells Henry that their father wants him to send money. Funds would be tight in Phelps until the harvest and their father George "has had none from Michigan." The family was not only in contact over half the continent, but was financially connected as well. We're mistaken if we assume that when people moved west, they cut their ties with family and went on their own.

Here's the letter:

Phelps May 19th

Respected Brother,

I take the present opportunity of informing you that our folks are well as usual. I am working at home this season. I have a couple of acres of peppermint planted &c. We have planted this season about six acres of mint nine acres corn six acres spring wheat potatoes oats sufficient &c.

As to stock they have five cows four yearlings and four calves and in the horse line Lucius thinks he has got a team. They have swopt the old big sorrel and a mare they had for a pair of Dun colored horses equally matched. As heavy as the old horse which makes a team, they being smart, and the big horse is yet on hand. They calculate to summer fallow about eighteen or twenty acres. There has been a very good spring so far for crops and there are prospects now for considerable fruit.

Our people are a going into the poultry line considerable this season. Forty or fifty chickens already and a quantity of eggs yet to hatch. Eleven young turkeys and two turkeys yet to hatch &c. &c.

Our folks have taken a girl about ten years old which they like very well. I believe which makes quite a help to the woman affairs. Dexter is yet in Michigan. I suppose William is a building a new house in the west village. Frederick is about here as usual. Frank is about Pecks yet. No news &c.

You requested us to send the Names Births &c. of the children. I will write them viz.

Alonzo F Ranney Born Sept 13, 1812
Lewis G Ranney Born March 10, 1815
Henry S Ranney Born March 5, 1817
Lucius Ranney Born April 12, 1819
Priscilla M Ranney Do Jan 19, 1822
Harrison Ranney Born March 4, 1824

Lyman A Ranney Born August 1, 1828
Lemuel S Ranney Born Jany 17, 1831
Anson B Ranney Do May 31, 1833

Mother says she calculates to send you two or three pairs of socks.

James King is about Vienna making pumps.

James Flower was married a few weeks ago.

Father wishes you to send him fifty or a hundred Dollars if you can as he has had none from Michigan and having some to make out he Requests &c. Money is very scarce here now probably will be till after harvest.

They thought if you could spare it till fall it would accommodate very much then they want to square up the horse and the stock line and other small debts. Write again soon and send if you send &c.

Yours Truly
L G Ranney

Letter #2

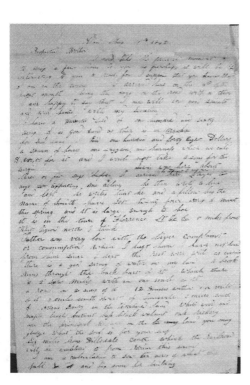

In May of 1842, 23-year old Lucius writes Henry of his arrival in Allen Michigan, after a 10-day journey from Phelps. He announces he has bought a quarter section (160 acres) of prime farmland for $148 cash and the wagon and team of horses he had used to make the trip. Lucius describes the property, listing the distances to neighbors and nearby towns, inventorying the trees and water on the parcel, and noting that the railroad will run only six miles from the property later in the year.

Lucius mentions that their brother Lewis came down to welcome him to Michigan, from his farm in St. Joseph County, about fifty miles away. Lucius also says their father is "very low" and that although their parents intend to move from New York to Michigan in the fall, he doesn't think they will. He is correct: their father George died a few months later. Their mother, Achsah Sears Ranney, lived another 27 years and, once the railroad was running in Michigan, spent much of her time traveling between Massachusetts, New York, and Michigan, visiting her children.

Lucius tells Henry he plans to plant winter wheat and gives the current prices for wheat, corn, and oats. He closes by asking Henry to write soon, and to send Massachusetts newspapers so he can keep up with events out east.

Allen May 15th 1842

Respected Brother

I now take the present moment to drop a few lines to you as perhaps it will be interesting to you to read, for I suppose that you know that I am in the woods. I arrived here on the fourth of the present month being ten days on the road with a team. I am happy to say that I am well in good spirits and well suited with my location.

I have a warrantee deed of one hundred sixty acres of as good land as there is in Michigan. For said land I paid one hundred and forty eight dollars, a span of horses, one wagon and harness which we calc $280.00 for it and I would not take a song for the bargain.

Lewis was here about three of four days before I arrived here. He thought I was here, stayed two days expecting me along. He then wrote a line and left. He writes that he and a fellow by the name of Smith have set twenty four acres of mint this spring and it is large enough to hoe. It is in the town of Florence St. Jo. Co. 5 miles from White Pigeon north I think.

Father was very low with a liver complaint or consumption when I left home. I have not heard from him since I left. The rest were well as usual.

There is a good spring of water on my land. A brook runs through the back part of it which there is two saw mills within one mile of it. A road on 2 sides of it. 12 houses within 1 1/2 mile of it. 9 miles south west of Jamesville. 3 miles south of Allens in the timbered land white wood and maple beech butnut bass black walnut oak hickory are the principal timber on the land. You may judge what the soil is for yourself. Six miles from Hillsdale Center which the railroad will be completed to from Adrian this season.

I am calculating to sow ten acres of wheat this fall and fix some for building. Our folks are expecting to move out here this fall but I don't think that they will. I stayed with Orren Ranney one night in Adrian. He is in the mercantile business and is a doing well I expect.

Wheat is worth 87 1/2 cents per bushel here oats 25 corn 31. I wish you would send the papers along here into the woods at least 1 or 2 a week so that I can pass of leisure time in a pleasant way. Direct yours to Sylvanus, Hillsdale Co. I have my board for $1.25 per week. I don't think of anything more to write just now. Give my respects to all inquiring friends. If you can solve this writing you will do well. Write as soon as convenient.

This from a Distant Brother

Lucius Ranney

Letter #3

Lucius tells Henry he has traded one of his lots of land for one with a better situation, which might mean that the land is better for farming or that it's closer to town. The new parcel has thirty-five improved acres, ready for planting. Lucius reports in detail how much he paid for the parcel and what he plans to do with the new land.

In addition to farming, Lucius has gone into the Potash business. Until settlers reached the treeless Great Plains, there were almost always forests to clear before the wheat could be planted. Potash, made by soaking wood ash in water and then evaporating the water in cast-iron pots, was often the first product settlers could ship back to Eastern markets. Lucius remarks that the land around Allen is filling up fast. Woodlands are becoming wheat fields, and the value of land will rise quickly as the last parcels are settled. Then Lucius gives his brother some advice: Henry should find a wife.

Allen April 30th 43
Henry Ranney

Dear Brother

I once more take my pen to write a few lines to inform you that I am well & ever have been in Michigan. I shall not apologize for not writing any sooner for I have not any except negligence to make. I suppose you are well are you not? I hear nothing in particular from you of late but receive papers from you quite often which I peruse with pleasure. I traded one of my lots of land the other day for a lot with 35 acres improved House &

Barn. I gave or rather agreed to give five Hundred Dollars in four yearly payments, the first next fall, & clear ten acres on the lot I let him have. I think the extra improvements are worth five Hundred Dollars & the situation of it is worth One Hundred Dollars more than the one I traded, so therefore you see that according to my estimation I have made $100. We have money enough due this fall in Phelps to make the first payment & shall with common luck raise enough wheat to pay the rest. I have six acres of wheat on the ground which bids fair for 100 bushels. I intend to clear 20 acres this summer & seed thirty to wheat. I have two as good lots of land for farming as there is in Michigan or anywhere else. If you doubt my word come out here and see which I hope you will this fall will you not?

As for Lewis I saw him a few weeks ago. He was well and is doing well I guess. He & his partner will have about 50 acres of mint to still this fall. You had better come out this fall & buy their oil. What is it worth now?

I wrote a letter home about two weeks since stating to our folks that I should probably be at home about the tenth of May. I suppose that they will move then to the West but shall write again today that I shall not return home until June for my business is such that I cannot leave at present. I want to plant about eight acres this spring & further- more I am in the Potash business with a partner. One of Mrs Baggerly's Son in Laws. We are a building a Pot-Ash this spring. We have made three tons & we find it profit- able therefore we intend to follow the business.

This part of the country is settling fast. Where there was forests one year ago the same surface is now waving with wheat. The cars will run to Hillsdale Center this summer, six miles east from where this child is & then you can come out here in a hurry if you please.

We have had a hard winter for the past one for this country. Grain is pretty well up. Wheat is worth 62 cents per bushel corn 50 oats 37 potatoes 25 &c.

I shall give you a little advice, that is a man of your cloth & business ought to have a wife. Why? Because you are at home at night then and nothing to trouble your mind but someone to cheer up your drooping spirits. But you are now a hunting up a horse and then you are in trouble to know who to take to this party that ball that ride this circus &c. But it is different with me. Sometimes I should be at home at night & sometimes in the woods to where night would overtake me I should be obliged to stay. Now I am con- tented where ever I am, with a wife I should be discontented under such circumstances. Therefore you see the disadvantage I should labor under with one. But I don't say that I shan't have one.

Enough on that head. I want you should write as soon as you receive this or put it off till after I go East. I shall go about the first of June. I should like to meet you there or somewhere else very much. I do not know when I shall go to Ashfield if ever, but think I shall in the course of a year or two. If you see any of Uncle Jesse's folks just ask them what part their girls live. When I am a traveling about I may go near them. If I do I should like to know it & go and see them. I have been through Medinah where I heard since one lived. Give my respects to all inquiring friends.

Yours in haste, Henry S. R.

Lucius Ranney

Excuse bad spelling writing &c.

Letter #4

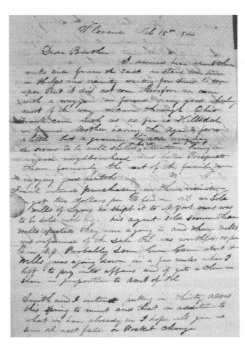

Lewis writes to Henry from Florence Michigan in February 1844. Lewis reports with amusement that the Mormons have been battling with the Methodists and others in Michigan, noting that it's nice to have "something going on." The Michigan economy is better off than western New York, Lewis tells Henry in closing. Wheat is worth five shillings (due to the scarcity of American coins, British Shillings were still in wide use), and Lewis is not yet tied down. When his partner Smith marries, Lewis intends to live with him rather than get his own place.

Florence Feb 15th 1844
Dear Brother

I arrived here about three weeks since from the East. We stayed some time in Phelps and vicinity waiting for snow to come upon. But it did not come, therefore we came with a wagon. We found very good wheeling most of the way. We came through Ohio. Frank came with us as far as Hillsdale. We found Mother having the ague & fever a little but a growing lighter every day. She seems to be well suited with her situation, being in a good neighborhood and better prospects than formerly. The rest of the family were enjoying good healths.

Frank intends purchasing in their vicinity. We got two dollars per lb for our oil we sold

Wells of Lyons. He shipped it to N. York, ours was to be sold with his. His agent sold sooner than Wells expected they were a going to and when Wells was informed of the sale oil was worth $4.00 per lb in NY. Probably some Gum Game about it. Wells was a going down in a few weeks when I left to pry into affairs and if he gets a clue we share in proportion to amt of oil.

Smith and I intend putting in thirty acres this spring to mint and that in addition to what we have already in I hope will give us some oil next fall for pocket change.

Lucius intends going to Grand River sometime in March I believe. He shall get something from that way this spring.

We are having great excitement about here again this winter. Methodists and Mormons are proselytizing considerably in this vicinity and something a doing with the other sects. The Mormons have gained a good many converts in this town and have organized a church. The sectarian preachers combine against the Mormons. But the Mormons having received challenges for discussions upon the Bible they accepted, which has made amusement for the hearer. Which is satisfactory to have something going on.

Wheat is worth 5/- per bushel. Times are better here than in New York. There has been no snow here this winter of any consequence. Smith my partner gets married in about two weeks. I shall live with him.

Nothing more. Yours respectfully,
L. G. Ranney
Write occasionally and send papers in any quantity.

Letter #5

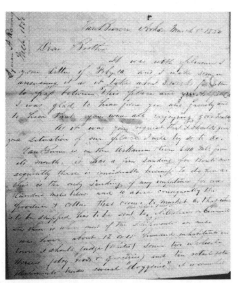

Younger brother Lyman writes Henry from Van Buren, Arkansas, in the Spring of 1850. He thanks his brother for writing, and says he is responding immediately because it takes three weeks for the mails between Arkansas and Ashfield. In response to Henry's questions, Lyman describes Van Buren and the commerce there. Although many have caught "California fever," Lyman lacks the funds to go farther west, but he does hope to move back to the north once he has made his fortune.

Lyman tells the story of a young boy who looked white, and who as a result was apparently worth less than other slave children. Lyman says he would like to bring the boy back to the north, "and let them see what some of the subjects are that are held in bondage." But, realizing that his abolitionist opinions are unwelcome in the South, Lyman reminds Henry that when he sends newspapers, it would be best to send no openly Free Soil papers.

After Lyman concludes his letter to Henry he writes a short note to his new sister-in-law, Maria. Although they have never met, Maria apparently wrote to Lyman along with Henry, admonishing him to be good. Lyman thanks her for the advice, and assures her that "fortunately I never was guilty of anything which I thought would degrade me or detract from my character."

Translation note: Doggery is a word dating from about 1830 for a low-class saloon or dive. Lyman puts quotes around it in his letter, suggesting the word and probably the places are a bit of a novelty for him.

Van Buren Arks. March 8th 1850

Dear Brother

It was with pleasure I recd your letter of Feb 10th and I make soon in answering it as it takes about three weeks for letters to pass between this place and Ashfield. I was glad to hear from you and family and to hear that you were all enjoying good health.

As it was your request that I should give you a situation of our place I will try so to do. Van Buren is on the Arkansas River 600 miles from its mouth. It has a fine landing for boats, consequently there is considerable business to do here as this is the only landing of any importance for one hundred miles below and 10 above. Consequently the produce and cotton that comes to market or that which is to be shipped has to be sent to this place if sent to New Orleans or Cincinnati, and there is where most of the shipments are made.

We have about 12 or 15 hundred inhabitants in town I should judge (Whites). Some two wholesale houses (dry goods & groceries) and ten retail establishments besides several "doggeries." It is somewhat mountainous in most parts of Ark. and therefore is not so productive as it otherwise would be. The climate is very mild, there not having been any snow here since I arrived. The weather at present is very delightful & warm. People are making gardens and some made garden two weeks ago.

The people in this place are much mixed. Some from the Southern States, some from Ohio & Indiana, and others from Va. N.J. And in fact from almost every state. Even from the old Bay State. There is two or three merchants here from Boston, been here about two years.

They have a very good society of young people here and as I get acquainted with them I like them very much.

Although the village people are as intelligent as they are in any country, it seems to be far different with the country people, for I think at least there is one in three of them that cannot write their own names. Consequently are ignorant and are harder to deal with than they would be otherwise, as they are so afraid of getting cheated.

Mr. Bishop has gone East after goods, intends going to Boston for the most of them. I told him to find Elisha Bassett while there if he could. I didn't know his address consequently could not direct him. I like merchandising very much so far and think that it will suit me well.

There are large numbers going to California this spring from this place and surrounding country. I have had the California fever but have got over it mostly, as it is not possible for me to get there under present circumstances. Slavery exists here in almost all forms. Some have a good master, others hard. Some slaves are black others are white. There is one boy around in town who is whiter than half the so called white children. He has very light colored hair, roman nose, and his features do not resemble a negro in the least. Yet this boy is a slave. He was sold since I have been here for 150$, being less than half what a black boy would have brought, or him if he was black. If I had plenty of money when I go north I would purchase him and take with me and let them see what some of the subjects are that are held in bondage.

I sent you 2 newspapers a few days since and will send one occasionally. I hope you will do likewise. It would not be best to send any Free Soil papers. Thinking of nothing of importance to write you at present I shall close as I am a going to write a few lines to your wife. Mrs. Bishop sends her love to you and wife. Hoping you will write soon, I now close.

I send my love to all our friends in Mass.

P.S. As regards Uncle Henry, I do not know his address nor cannot find out as there is no one knows where he is exactly. He never lived in V.B. but lived formerly about 30 miles from the mouth. He was in the habit of using liquor to some extent, but I understand he had left off when he returned last fall.

Affectionately yrs
Lyman A Ranney

Dear Sister

Although I never had the privilege of a personal acquaintance with you, still it does not seem that you are a perfect stranger to me as I have heard Mother speak of you so often. I am glad to hear from you and am thankful for the good advice you and Henry have put forth in your letter, although fortunately I never was guilty of anything which I thought would degrade me or detract from my character. I am glad to hear that you are all well and hope that I may yet see you all in Mass. Perhaps the time may be years distant. As it is getting late and for want of room I will have to close these few lines to you. I hope to hear from you and Henry often.

From your Brother
Lyman

Lucius Ranney's farm was located south of the town of Allen, Michigan. His two 80-acre parcels are at the bottom center of this 1880 map, just above the lake.

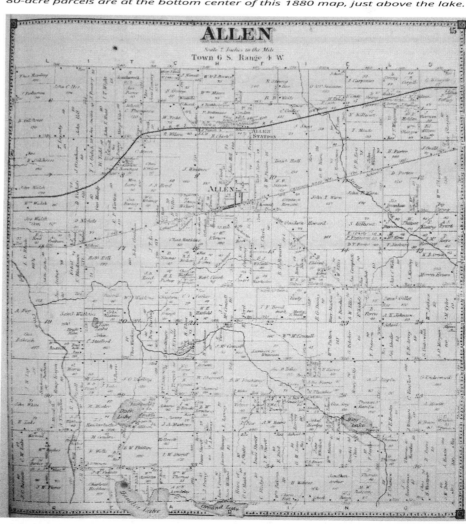

Chapter Five:
Commons, Mills, Corporations

The Industrial Revolution not only changed America's economy and spurred the growth of cities; it changed the way Americans relate to the natural environment. In this chapter we trace changes in our ideas of what the environment is for, and who it's for.

Along with their old-world ideas about culture, farming, and social organization, the English men and women who colonized North America brought with them a legal tradition known as the Common Law. English Common Law is a set of legal principles dating back to the Middle Ages. In this tradition the source of the law and its authority are not royal decrees or legislative acts, but rather the accumulation of judges' decisions on specific cases. Murder, for example, is a Common Law crime in Britain. It never required an Act of Parliament to declare murder illegal. Government can influence the Common Law, however; as it did when the British Parliament changed the mandatory sentence for murder from the death penalty to life imprisonment. The interaction between legislation and Common Law is important in American Environmental History because throughout most of the nineteenth and early twentieth centuries our relationship with our environment has been shaped partly by legislative deliberations, but more often by routine court decisions that have created a series of legal precedents regarding property, usage rights, and liability.

The relationship modern Americans have with our physical environment and America's culture of large corporations that often seem above the law actually developed together, because many of the most successful early corporations radically changed their physical environments. The Common Law America inherited from England contained a long list of precedents that guided judges in arbitrating between the claims of people whose interests conflicted. Some of these precedents dated back to the Roman Empire, giving judges clear guidance in deciding the rights and responsibilities of individuals. But society wasn't made up only of individuals. Even though Americans had left behind the royalty and hereditary nobility of British society, there were still some tasks that seemed too big for individuals. Towns raised militia when needed, and the national government commanded an army and a navy and collected customs duties at ports. The States ran criminal and civil courts. But who was going to build colleges, hospitals, and bridges? As America grew there were institutions and services that society needed but that no individual had the resources to create on their own.

Incorporation

Early America's answer was incorporation. Corporations during the colonial period had been quasi-public organizations given a royal charter to do a particular job. The Virginia Company and the Massachusetts Bay Company had both been royally chartered corporations. They earned profits for their shareholders, but they also had, or at least claimed to have, an important social function that transcended mere business. Without this social dimension, businesses—even very large ones—were normally organized as partnerships or sole proprietorships. State legislatures in early America continued the English tradition and chartered corporations to do particular tasks in the public interest. Colonial governments began this practice very early in our history, when the Massachusetts legislature established Harvard College in 1636 and then chartered the Harvard Corporation, America's first corporation, in 1650.

Corporate influence on the environment begins with this first American corporation. In 1640, the Massachusetts

Boston, 1838. The competing bridges are on the right.

legislature gave Harvard a license to run a ferry between Boston and Charlestown across the Charles River, to raise money to operate the college. When the State of Massachusetts granted a corporate charter to the Charles River Bridge Company in 1785, to build the first bridge across the river, the new charter specified that the bridge company had to pay Harvard £200 per year to compensate the college for the revenue the old ferry operation would lose.

The Charles River Bridge was a privately operated toll bridge. Although it had originally been conceived as a public corporation that would provide a social benefit, the bridge company was wildly successful. The corporation had been capitalized at $50,000, meaning that $50,000 had been raised to build the bridge by selling shares to investors. Once built, the bridge collected $824,798 in tolls between 1786 and 1827. Although the original plan had been to eliminate the tolls once the bridge had paid for itself, the shareholders decided to continue profiting from their monopoly. So they voted to continue charging tolls and paying the profits out to their shareholders.

Enriching a few shareholders at everyone else's expense was not what Massachusetts legislators had intended when they had granted the corporation a charter to build a bridge that would monopolize river crossing. But although the Bridge Company had violated the spirit of their agreement with the State, it hadn't actually broken any laws. So the legislature chartered a new corporation, the Warren Bridge Company, to build a second bridge across the river next to the Charles River Bridge. The new charter specified that the Warren Bridge Company would only be allowed to collect tolls for six years or until the bridge paid for itself, whichever came first. Then ownership would revert to the Commonwealth and the bridge would be toll-free.

The Charles River Bridge Company sued the Warren Bridge Company, claiming their 1785 charter granted them a perpetual monopoly on traffic across the river. Charles River Bridge revenues disappeared, as travelers chose to pay the lower tolls on the new bridge. The lawsuit failed in Massachusetts courts, and the plaintiffs took their complaint all the way to the U.S. Supreme Court. In spite of hiring famous orator Daniel Webster to argue their case, the Charles River Bridge Company lost. The court's decision reflected the judges' belief that the profits of the corporation and the interests of its shareholders were less important—and legally came second—to the State's authority to charter corporations to meet public needs. Even so, the tremendous profits taken by Charles River Bridge shareholders and their ability to push their lawsuit to the highest court signaled the beginning of a change in the way corporations viewed their role in society and the responsibilities that went with their public charters.

Streams and Mills

Although by chartering a bridge corporation to connect Boston and Charlestown, Massachusetts had legislated a solution to an environmental problem, most early environmental issues were smaller scale. So they were handled locally, by reference to Common Law. In preindustrial America, lakes, rivers, and streams were considered community resources. This was another inheritance from feudal England, where peasants had shared fields owned by noble landlords and had grazed their animals on common pastures. Early New England towns and cities were often built around a central Common which served as a meeting-place for militia as well as a pasture. Like town Commons where everybody could let their animals graze, rivers, streams, and coastal fisheries were shared resources. Waterways were an important means of transportation; often the only way to get people and supplies to and from remote backcountry settlements. And rivers were vital food sources for many European Americans, just as they had been for the Indians before the colonists arrived.

Shad was known as "the fish that fed the nation's founders."

Fish like Alewife, Herring, Shad, and Atlantic Salmon migrated from the ocean into rivers to spawn each spring. The annual run happened at just the right time of year, when stores of food were running out, and provided a common resource that was open to all. Fish from rivers and lakes were often an important part of subsistence for poorer Americans. The annual runs were a major source of springtime nutrition for native and Euro-Americans for several centuries. But from the earliest period of European settlement, there were other uses for rivers that could conflict with free travel and fishing. Colonial and early American settlements used a lot of timber for building and grew a lot of wheat for home use and for sale. So every settlement needed mills.

Atlantic Salmon.

When towns were chartered in colonial times and in the early national period, organizers usually offered a reward of free land to anyone willing to start a grist mill or a sawmill in the new town. Heavy mill machinery would have to be carried to the town-site and assembled, and then operating the mill required some expertise and took time away from building a house and clearing fields. So it made sense to offer some type of bounty to attract millers, since everybody in town would need lumber and flour, but no indivudual needed or could afford to build a private mill.

The idea that some projects were too big

Early nineteenth-century fish traps, used during annual shad runs.

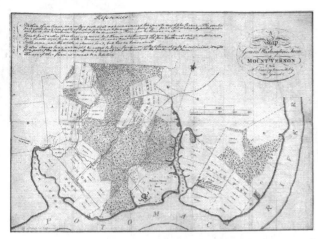

1801 map of Mount Vernon, drawn by George Washington.

for everybody to do themselves and that it made more sense to share expensive, seldom-used tools is ancient. Today economists call these types of goods natural monopolies. Sawmills and grist mills, although they were owned and run by individuals, clearly existed for the common good. No single farmer had enough wheat or needed enough lumber to justify building a private mill for their sole use. And no miller could afford the expense or expect to recover his investment without the market provided by the rest of the town. So millers received a special incentive, and in return the mills would be open to everyone at an affordable rate. There was a social contract involved in this activity that everyone understood.

The earliest homes in a new township were usually log cabins. But it's difficult to build a large structure with logs. Early town records usually show a rapid shift from log houses and barns to frame construction as soon as a sawmill opened in a town. Sawing lumber for a small project could be done by hand, if necessary. But driving a large millstone required more power. Millwheels could be turned by animals, but the job was better done by water power. So any township that included a stream with a decent fall of water was considered a prime location for a settlement.

People who ran sawmills and grist mills were seen as providing a necessary service to the whole society. The mills were private in the sense that they were owned by individuals rather than by the town. But they were public in the sense that they were open to everybody, rather than just existing to serve a single family's needs. Millers were also often involved in combining local farmers' harvests and selling flour to cities back east. So they provided a widely-needed public service, because very few individual families in the northeast and the Yankee west produced enough grain by themselves to justify the expense of traveling east to sell their flour. This was different in the South, where large plantations often operated their own mills. Planters like George Washington and Thomas Jefferson often tried to build self-sufficient little societies on their properties, with their own mills, workshops, and even small factories. The self-contained nature of plantations is one reason the story of industrialization takes place in the Northeast and Yankee West rather than in the South. Outside the plantation economy, people needed mills and millers needed to be open to the public in order to have enough work to be profitable. So the benefit went both ways.

The streams and rivers that the millers used for power did not belong to them. At some township sites, a river's volume and fall were enough that a miller only needed to divert a little water into a channel called a millrace, to power the mill wheel. In other places, a partial or full dam was required to generate enough force to turn the wheel. When a miller needed to build a dam and change the natural flow of the stream, he was responsible and legally liable for the effects of his dam on people upstream and downstream from him.

Dam Breaking

New England millers often took down their dams during spring freshets and fish runs.

With so many people depending on rivers for transportation, food, irrigation and drinking water, changes in a river's flow were often controversial. A mill pond might flood a farmer's field upstream, or cut off water to a farm or another mill downstream. A dam might prevent fish from running upstream to their spawning grounds, endangering not only this year's food supply but future fish populations. The issue was considered so serious and the stakes so high that it was actually legal in early America for people who felt they'd been injured by a mill's dam to go ahead and break the dam. If their farmland had been flooded or if the flow of water to a downstream farm or mill was cut off, the injured party could break the dam and restore the flow of water while the dispute was being settled in court. People were legally entitled to restore the stream to its original condition until society decided what was fair for everyone. The common law approach to water rights was so ancient that it was expressed by a Latin phrase used in the Roman empire two thousand years earlier, *aqua currit et debet currere, ut currere solebat*: water flows and ought to flow, as it has customarily flowed. Any manmade change to a river's natural state could be challenged, because everyone had equal rights to the river.

In many places, mill dams were also seasonal structures that would be partially broken each year to allow freshets of snowmelt to pass by without flooding and damaging the area. Dams were also taken down to allow the fish to run upstream in the spring. And flour or saw milling was seasonal work in many small towns, so mill races and ponds didn't need to be permanent and always in use.

In early American towns, mills and their dams were well-understood technologies that had existed for many generations, authorized by the townspeople and used for the common good. The mills and their technology were part of a social system that emphasized their status as

Robert Owen's mill city at New Lanarck.

shared resources for community use. There was a reciprocal give and take between people who had different interests in the society, in social customs and in common law. Millers were given special incentives to move to new towns and help them grow. In return, they were responsible for keeping the mill running and available to everybody, and for responding to their neighbors when they changed the flow of streams in ways that caused problems. In return, the millers got what amounted to a local monopoly on sawing wood and grinding flour. Although other millers weren't specifically barred from opening competing mills, there was only so much need, and there was only so much water power. But there were always new towns needing millers, so common customs and common sense were effective ways to regulate early mills.

Textile Factories

But new technology was developed and as the pace of change accelerated, this common law, common sense social contract started to break down. One of the specific events that accelerated this change was a visit to Scotland in 1810 and 1811, when a pair of prosperous Boston merchants named Nathan Appleton and Francis Cabot Lowell toured the textile mills at New Lanark. These woolen mills on the River Clyde were run by an industrialist named Robert Owen, and were the largest completely water-powered mills in Great Britain and probably the world. Owen's textile operation employed so many people that the company had needed to build an entire community around it to house the millworkers.

Appleton and Lowell's mill city at Lowell.

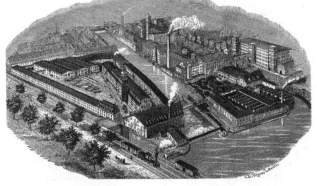

Robert Owen and his partners had bought the mills from David Dale, Owen's father-in-law. Sensitive to the negative social changes that industrial growth had brought to other parts of Britain, Owen had built schools for the children of his workers, and social organizations for the workers. He put an end to the long-standing custom of forcing workers to buy only from the company store and tried to make New Lanark a real, living town. Owen's partners objected to his philanthropy, claiming that healthy, happy, well-educated workers didn't really boost the bottom line. Rather than fight with them, Owen simply bought his partners out.

Appleton and Lowell returned to America and immediately began the Boston Manufacturing Company in 1813 on the Charles River in Waltham, Massachusetts. At that time there were twenty-three other mills on the Charles, but the BMC was something different. Appleton and Lowell's mill was a completely water-powered textile factory on the model of New Lanark. The Boston Associates followed Owen's example, and began building complete industrial cities in New England. Nashua, Manchester, and Concord on the Merrimack River grew substantially with the new textile industry. Lawrence and Lowell were built from the ground up as factory towns. But the Boston Associates not only created cities and filled them with industrial wage workers. They changed the way Americans understood their environment.

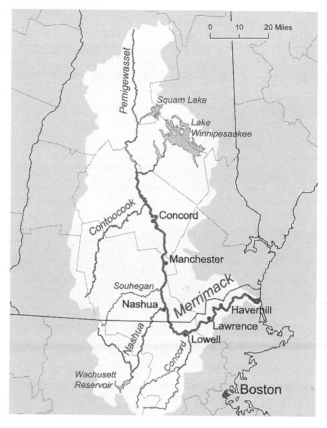

Factory Girls

The BMC's textile mills employed mostly young women, aged 15 to 30. Between 1840 and 1860, the number of mill girls working in the Massachusetts textile industry rose from about ten thousand to over a hundred thousand. For context, the population of New England's largest city, Boston, was about 93,000 in 1840 and 178,000 in 1860. By 1848, Lowell was the largest industrial city in America.

When the BMC opened their first mill, only seven out of a hundred Americans lived in

cities. By the middle of the nineteenth century, the nation's urban population was approaching twenty percent, with a lot of help from the mill girls. Some of the women were immigrants, but most had come from farm families. A hundred thousand young women moved to the city to work twelve hours a day in the textile mills. In spite of harsh work conditions and low pay, many of these women were experiencing personal freedom for the first time, and liking it. Most never went back to the countryside. As cities like Lowell, Lawrence, and Manchester grew around the mills, they created a new American population group, the urban wage-worker. The mill girls and other factory workers lived a different life and had very different concerns from those of the families they'd left behind in the countryside. Although they joined the new labor movement and were often critical of the mills they worked in, the mill girls' lives became tied to the wellbeing of the industry that employed them.

Too Big to Fail

The creation and continued existence of new cities like Lowell depended entirely on the Boston Manufacturing Company's financial fortunes. Prosperity for Lowell's citizens was tied to the success of the business that paid their wages. The BMC was too big to fail. Over time, it was only natural for the city's dependence on its creator and main employer to change the way people understood the public good.

At the height of its power, the BMC controlled the Merrimack River from its source in Lake Winnipesaukee to its outflow in the Atlantic. The Boston Associates decided how much water would be let out of the lake and built dams to control the flow along the entire river so that all of the Merrimack's water power was available to run BMC textile factories. River transportation, fishing, and all other competing uses of the Merrimack's water were basically set aside.

Another example of limitation of corporate liability was visible when the textile industry declined and the BMC abandoned the cities it had created to their fates.

How did this happen? How did one corporation get control over what only a generation earlier had been understood by all to be a shared resource, open to everyone? There was no bill presented to Congress. No elected representatives voted for this change. If the issue had been debated in the legislature, things might have gone differently. Instead, the change happened very slowly and under the radar, through a series of legal changes stemming from court decisions and changes in contract law.

It's important to remember that the public benefited from early corporations. That's why the community allowed them to inconvenience or even injure individuals from time to time, in the same way towns allowed the local miller to occasionally flood a field, as long as he compensated the farmer for his loss. It was an issue of the public good coming before the private good. And corporations had public responsibilities: in exchange for special treatment, usually some form of a natural or legislated monopoly, the corporation was expected to act in the public interest. So how did it all change between then and now?

The first step was a gradual shift in the interpretation of the mill laws. In every state there were laws that regulated how disputes over water rights would be addressed by the courts. Before the nineteenth century, the common law approach to water rights had been expressed by that Latin phrase, "water flows and ought to flow, as it has customarily flowed." In Massachusetts, the mill laws dated from 1713, and they only allowed the property of other landowners to be compromised by mills "for the publick good." But as time went on and case after case was brought before Massachusetts courts, judges began to rethink the phrase public good. As the users of water power grew from village grist mills to textile factories, the judges began to see industry itself as a public good. By the time the Boston Associates were building entire cities from the ground up and providing employment for hundreds of thousands, it was difficult to argue there wasn't a public interest in their success, even if the profits of the enterprise were restricted to just a few shareholders.

Slater Mill, est. 1793, Pawtucket, was a partnership, not a corporation.

Because textile factories used water power, even if it was on a much larger scale, Massachusetts judges regulated them using mill laws designed to regulate village sawmills and grist mills. Not only did the scale of the BMC's operations make this legal treatment inappropriate, the judges lost sight of the fact that the Boston Manufacturing Company was a private corporation operating for the profit of its shareholders, while village mills had operated for the public good. As a result of a series of judgments, mostly in lower courts, the BMC was allowed to redefine its relationship with society and the environment. And, so slowly that almost no one noticed at the time, the nature of corporations themselves changed, and the idea of a social contract for the public good was lost.

When Samuel Slater had opened America's first textile mill in 1793 on the Blackstone River in Pawtucket, Rhode Island, he had organized his company as a partnership. But as business opportunities grew, the idea of incorporation changed. Between 1800 and 1809, fifteen corporate charters were given to Massachusetts manufacturers. In the next ten years, the number jumped to 133. Corporations gradually stopped presenting themselves as public-spirited foundations operating institutions like hospitals and colleges in the public interest. They became more like the business corporations we know today, whose missions are understood to be building share price and returning a profit to their shareholders. But because incorporation had once been about providing public services in exchange for special privileges, the new corporations frequently retained their special privileges, even after they had stopped providing public services.

Evading Responsibility

Along with legislated monopoly, one of the special privileges corporations enjoyed was limited liability. Instead of being responsible for all the damages that might be caused by a textile mill, a shareholder only risked the amount he invested. This allowed businesses to take bigger risks, since the worst that could happen in case of a disaster would be that the company would declare bankruptcy. Shareholders would lose only the money they had spent to buy company shares; their other assets could not be taken to compensate the victims of their company's risky behavior.

By measuring and selling mill-power rather than water, the BMC avoided confronting the long-standing tradition that rivers could not be privately owned.

It's important to remember that the reinterpretation of business law and contracts that allowed these changes to happen was not done by elected representatives in legislative debate, but by lawyers and judges who were often friends, relatives, and investors of the new textile industrialists. They shared not only an interest in the mills' success, but a cultural orientation that made it easy to see the the textile industry itself as a public good to be protected.

The most environmentally damaging change caused by the New England textile industry, though, was the gradual elimination the idea of common resources. First, they separated the old mill laws from an idea of common good, and used them to arbitrate property disputes of people who owned land beside rivers. They subverted the common law understanding of

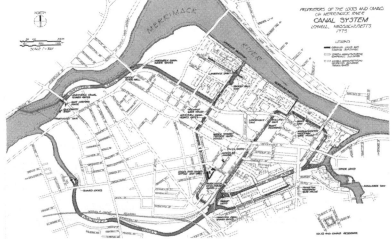

equal rights to water resources and shared responsibility for their upkeep. Then they actually eliminated the idea that waterways were a community resource, so the flow of the river could be treated as a commodity that could be bought and sold by individuals. They did this by creating a water power company called the Proprietors of the Locks and Canals (PLC) which invented a concept called mill-power, that they sold to the mills.

Mill-power was a number that measured the work that could be done by river water pushing the textile factories' wheels. Although it was a long-standing tradition that running water should not be considered private property, mill-power was just a measurement invented by the PLC for accounting purposes. There were no laws preventing the PLC from selling mill-power to the BMC factories along the Merrimack River.

The immediate effect of reducing the physical river to an input into an accounting calculation was that the rest of society who had no interest in buying mill-power was no longer involved in these transactions. Society hadn't been prevented from participating, it just made no sense for them to participate. As a result, everyone who didn't own a millwheel along the river suddenly had no access to the river and no say in its use. Worse, once a market price had been established even people with riverside property could be bought out, and effectively silenced forever.

There were never any bills introduced into the Massachusetts or New Hampshire legislatures, allowing citizens to debate whether the Merrimack River should be handed over to the corporation begun by Nathan Appleton and Francis Cabot Lowell. Appleton himself was elected to the U.S. Congress in 1842, and although Lowell died in 1817 at age 42, his son Francis Cabot Lowell Jr. was a U.S. Congressman and a Federal Judge. In 1850, the BMC's textile empire earned $14,000,000 in annual revenue, which was half the Gross Domestic Product of Massachusetts and New Hampshire. BMC profits were high, because they were the biggest supplier of cotton fabric in the market and because they were able to control their costs by keeping the mill girls' wages low. After an unsuccessful strike, mill workers formed the Lowell Female Labor Reform Association to fight for higher wages, lower rents in company-owned boarding houses, and a ten-hour day. A Legislative Committee looked into the mill girls' demands and decided it was not the state's responsibility to set work hours. Another important source of BMC profits was the low price of raw cotton, which of course was produced by people who didn't have to be paid at all.

When the shad and the salmon were no longer able to swim up the Merrimack River to breed, New Englanders lost

Lowell's factory girls began organizing in 1836. Women weren't admitted to national labor unions until the late 1860s.

a food source that had sustained generations every spring. The BMC was sued for damages by fishermen and residents along the river. In 1848 the corporation settled these lawsuits with payments totaling $26,000 to the plaintiffs. In return for a one-time cash payment, the plaintiffs and their descendants relinquished all future claims against the corporation. In other words, for $26,000 the destruction of a major New England fishery was settled once and for all. The fish were gone for good, but the only people compensated were a handful of plaintiffs in a single lawsuit. Since the case was settled, no one else would be allowed to sue for damages in the future, even though a resource that had always been available for common use had disappeared. This result illustrates not only how much power goes along with owning half the economy of two states, but also how difficult it can be setting a one-time economic value on long-term environmental changes.

Was the destruction of the habitat of the salmon, shad, and of the other species that depended on those fish worth $26,000? Was the elimination of a major seasonal food source for rural working-class people in the region worth $26,000? How long would it take until people had spent $26,000 buying food to replace the fish they could no longer catch in the river? No one knew, because the questions were never asked. The public had become divided into groups that didn't share the same interests. Whether there were fish in the river wasn't a question that really concerned factory girls or many other residents of the Lowell or Lawrence, whose lives now revolved around urban wage-workers' concerns such as work hours, rent in company dormitories, prices at the company store, and factory conditions. For the first time in America there was a population of working people that was permanently separated from direct contact with the land, and from the people who lived and worked on it. As we'll see in later chapters, this split of the American working class into urban and rural groups with different concerns had a profound impact on both social justice and the environment.

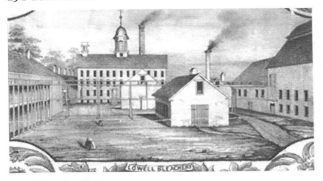

The Lowell Bleachery, 1832. Even some textile mills found they could only use river water to dye dark colors.

Pollution

In addition to privatizing the Merrimack River, the textile industry polluted it. In a sense, it didn't matter that the fish could no longer run up the river. They would not have been able to survive the water. By the middle of the nineteenth century, the BMC's mills and bleacheries were producing over fifty million yards of colored and printed fabric. The residue from those processes included dyes, bleaches, sulfuric acid, lime, and arsenic. Since there was no law against it, these residues were all dumped into the river. It was well-known that the running water of streams and rivers purified waste thrown into them, although no one really understood why. Unfortunately, the mills and the new cities the BMC had created overwhelmed the Merrimack's ability to renew itself.

Fish were killed up to two miles downstream from the mills' outlets. A state commission advised against drinking river water downstream from Lowell on the Merrimack and pronounced the Nashua River unfit for drinking along its entire length. But the commissioners, pressured by their industrial sponsors, concluded that cleaning up the river or preventing further contamination would be too costly.

Although the Lowell mills and their canal power system had been meticulously engineered, the same could not be said for the city the BMC created. As late as the 1870s, Lowell had no general sewage system. Cesspools leaked into the ground water, contaminating wells scattered throughout the city that provided Lowell's drinking water. Deaths in Lowell from typhoid fever, a water-borne disease, peaked in the 1870s, and exceeded typhoid deaths in Boston through the end of the century, even though by 1900 Boston had five times the population. In 1878 the Massachusetts legislature was forced to respond, and passed "An Act Relative to the Pollution of Rivers, Streams, and Ponds Used as Sources of Water Supply." However, bowing to industry pressure, the lawmakers exempted the Merrimack River from the law's provisions.

Externalities and Alternatives

The New England textile industry is usually remembered in history books as an enormous achievement. The Boston Manufacturing Company was wildly successful, and created a model for American industrialism. Some of that praise is deserved. Nathan Appleton and Francis Cabot Lowell, and the men who led the BMC after them, pioneered industrial organization and built cities for New England and fortunes for themselves. But often when we celebrate progress we forget the cost.

In January, 1860, the five story Pemberton Mill in Lawrence collapsed with about 800 workers inside. The business had recently been sold and building filled with newer, heavier machines. 700 looms had been updated, and a business that had been near failing seemed to have been

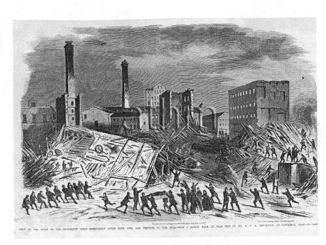

Collapse of the Pemberton Mill, January 10, 1860.

turned around with great success.

145 workers, mostly women, were killed in the collapse and 166 seriously injured. In an investigation after the accident, it was found the collapse had been the result of preventable factors such as the overloading of the floors with heavy equipment, overcrowding, and even gross negligence in the construction of the original mill buildings.

The disaster rallied some activists in the fight for workplace safety. But there were never any consequences for the people who owned and ran the factory. Life just went on. The Pemberton Mill's owner bought out his partner and built a new mill on the site of the old one. After his death, the new mill was inherited by the owner's sons. The building is still a landmark of Lawrence.

Even if we set aside disasters such as the Pemberton Mill collapse, how much of the success and profit attributed to the Boston Manufacturing Company and the other mills of the Merrimack River Valley was the result of not having to count the costs their operations imposed on the environment and on people like Northern mill girls and Southern slaves who had been written out of the equation? In a sense, the privatization of profits and socialization of costs that allowed the textile industry to dominate the New England economy was just another special privilege given to a corporation by society, in spite of the broken social contract that no longer asked the corporation for something of comparable social value in return. If we really accounted for the social and environmental costs, then how profitable was the Boston Manufacturing Company really? We'll come back to this idea, which economists call externality, in later chapters.

The development of the New England textile industry is an event that helps us see how subtle changes in laws and customs accumulated to create the world of global corporatism we live in today. Through a combination of becoming too big to fail and slowly changing the way the law understood the ideas of common resources and social responsibility, corporate industrialists turned the waters of one of New England's most valuable natural resources into a steady flow of profits for the BMC and its owners. Changes begun in the New England textile industry have led us directly to the ways we understand corporations, shared resources, and social responsibility today. But we shouldn't conclude that the way things ended up was inevitable. It was the result of hundreds of decisions, big and small, that people made along the way. To illustrate that, let's return to the beginning of this story, to Robert Owen.

Robert Owen organized a modern industrial city from the ground up in New Lanarck. Appleton and Lowell learned from Owen that social engineering on a grand scale was possible, and they came back to New England and followed Owen's example in Waltham and then along the Merrimack River. What did Owen do? Owen became the father of the British cooperative movement. In addition to being a successful, entrepreneur and capitalist, Owen promoted a system of corporate welfare that his critics, then and now, call socialist.

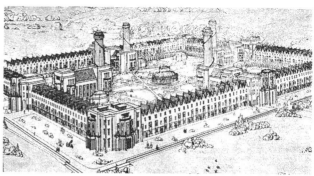

Robert Owen's vision for New Harmony, 1825.

Robert Owen tried to improve the society his father-in-law had created around the mills, by building schools and taking care of the health and welfare of his workers. New Lanark became a model of humane industrialism and socially responsible urban planning. But that wasn't enough for Owen. After his success in Scotland, Owen wondered how much farther he could go. So he sold his interest in the mills and moved to Indiana, where he founded a cooperative community called New Harmony. Like Appleton and Lowell, Robert Owen seems to have had an "Aha!" moment, when he realized how much power he held to change society and perhaps even to change people. But unlike the Boston Associates, who built a textile empire that made them millions, Owen chose to do something different with that power. Robert Owen's decision suggests that as hard as they may sometimes be to see, history often comes down to a series of human choices.

Further Reading

Sven Beckert, *Empire of Cotton, A Global History*. 2014.

Benita Eisler, ed., *The Lowell Offering: Writings By New England Mill Women (1845-1940)*. 1997.

Morton Horwitz, *The Transformation of American Law, 1780-1860*. 1977.

Ted Steinberg, *Nature, Incorporated*. 1991

Supplement: Radicalism in Heavy Prose

Tracing the way our relationship with the environment changed during industrialization is complicated by the fact that the changes cut across several fields of study that are usually quite separate. Scholars are often admonished to stay inside their disciplines, and most readers of Environmental History have little interest in digging into law books. But some of the most important insights into early American environmental change, it turns out, came from a Harvard Law professor named Morton Horwitz.

Horwitz published his ideas in 1977, in a thick volume called *The Transformation of American Law, 1780-1860*. The most important legal changes in early American history, Horwitz announced, had not resulted from legislative debate and democratic deliberation. On the contrary, "By 1820," Horwitz said, "the process of common law decision making had taken on many of the qualities of legislation. As judges began to conceive of common law adjudication as a process of making and not merely discovering legal rules, they were led to frame general doctrines based on a self-conscious consideration of social and economic policies."

That's a complicated way of saying that the most important legal changes affecting social and especially economic development were made not by elected representatives of the people, but from the bench by judges who were becoming aware of the important role they played in shaping society. In fact, Horwitz says, "By changing the rules and disguising the changes in the complexities of technical legal doctrine, the facade of economic security [could] be maintained even as new property [was] allowed to sweep away the old." Again, a complicated way of saying that the judges were able to gradually, one case at a time, reorganize American economic life around new corporate forms of property at the expense of an older tradition of common use rights and shared responsibilities.

This is a radical claim with far-reaching implications. Unfortunately, like the law itself, Horwitz's book is extremely difficult. So it's rarely read by anyone but Legal History graduate students. Luckily, in the late 1980s, Horwitz advised a grad student named Ted Steinberg, whose 1989 dissertation applied Horwitz's insights on law to environmental change in the early industrial revolution. The result is Steinberg's book, *Nature, Incorporated*.

Steinberg begins by explaining that "industrial capitalism is not only an economic system, but a system of ecological relations as well." Steinberg builds on Horwitz's explanation of legal change to show what basically amounts to a sneaky hijacking by early industrialists of common law and common sense attitudes toward ownership, creating confusion of public and private good. Water flowing in streams and rivers had always been a common resource, available to everyone. But during industrialization, Steinberg says, it became "commonly assumed, even expected, that water should be tapped, controlled, and dominated in the name of progress," and that the rewards of this control could legitimately be claimed by the few, to the exclusion of the many. This was a big change, and it opened the door for the modern world.

Steinberg tells the story of the rise of the Boston Manufacturing Company. Steinberg's book is important because it applies Morton Horwitz's very complex interpretation of legal change to the environment, and because it makes the story accessible to many more readers. But though harder to follow, Horwitz's conclusions were actually more radical than Steinberg's. Horwitz concluded his *Transformation* by describing the "rise of legal formalism" in the 1840s and 50s. "If a flexible, instrumental conception of law was necessary" to promote economic development, Horwitz says, "it was no longer needed once the major beneficiaries...had obtained the bulk of their objectives." In fact, just the opposite.

The law needed to become, and it needed to be seen as, "self-contained, apolitical, and inexorable." Having used the law to get to power, Horwitz says, the ruling class made justice a blind, impersonal statue as a way of "disguising and suppressing the inevitably political and redistributive functions of law." Horwitz claimed recent historians were "more concerned with finding evidence of governmental intervention than they were in asking in whose interest these regulations were forged." And he suggested the cover-up had been deliberate: "Change brought about through technical legal doctrine can more easily disguise underlying political choices [than] subsidy through the tax system." Horwitz concluded "there is reason to suppose" that this "was not simply an abstract effort to avoid political contention but that it entailed more conscious decisions about who would bear the burdens of economic growth." That is, America's most important Legal Historian said that throughout American History the law has been used by the powerful to get what they want and to shift the cost to the powerless. It's something to think about.

Completion of the transcontinental railway cut travel time from New York to California from 110 days to 10.

Chapter Six: Transportation

The transportation revolution in the United States began with Americans taking advantage of features of the natural environment to move people and things from place to place. Then a series of technological changes allowed transportation to advance to a point where machines have effectively conquered distance. People can almost effortlessly travel to anywhere in the world and ship raw materials and products across a global market.

But this technology is not ubiquitous, and it's not democratic. As a famous science fiction writer once said, the future is already here, it's just not very evenly distributed. Modern transportation is controlled to a great extent by large corporations, but it's depended on by everyone. And transportation technology itself requires specific conditions: abundant, cheap, portable energy in the form of fossil fuels, and public infrastructure created by our own and foreign governments, that even those large corporations depend on but don't control.

When we think of transportation, it's natural to think first about going places. Getting on a plane in one hemisphere and getting off on the other side of the world is a life-changing opportunity which was not available to most people as little as a generation ago. But more crucial to our daily lives is the cargo from the other side of the world that reaches us quickly in the holds of jets and more slowly but in almost unimaginable volume in containers on ships. This transportation of foods, raw materials, and finished goods makes our current lifestyle possible.

So although even the early stages of the transportation revolution allowed people like seventy-year old Achsah Ranney, from Chapter Five's Supplement, to travel regularly between her children's homes in Massachusetts, New York, and Michigan, the more significant change was the ability of her sons and other Americans to move goods from place to place. The ability to effectively ship food and other goods to where they were needed allowed people to stay put, and even to concentrate themselves in cities in a way they had never been able to do before. The growth of eastern cities depended just as much on the transportation revolution as the building of new cities in the west.

As we've already seen, Americans have made amazing journeys with very primitive methods of transportation. The people who crossed Beringia and settled North and South America were able to cover startlingly long distances on foot. Human and animal power has been used extensively throughout American history, and is still used today to reach remote areas off the grid. But it's clear that improvements in transportation technology have been some of the most powerful drivers of change in our history. And they've certainly changed our relationship with the American environment.

Technological improvements to ocean-going ships in the fifteenth century made European colonialism possible in the first place. Ships got bigger, faster, and safer. More people and goods could leave the safety of coastal waters and cross the oceans, and the places the ships connected became centers of trade, population, and wealth. This pattern of growth repeated as new technologies were developed to help Americans expand across the continent.

American colonists depended on trade with England and with the sugar planters of the West Indies to make their outposts in New England and Virginia successful. But between the Revolution and the War of 1812, relations between the new nation and Britain were tense and trade suffered. If it hadn't found a way to ship people and goods to and from the frontier, America would have remained a coastal nation, focused on ports like Boston, New York, Philadelphia, and Charleston. The barely-remembered Whiskey Rebellion of 1791, when George Washington led American troops against American farmers in western Pennsylvania, was really about transportation. Farmers over the Appalachian Mountains couldn't haul wagonloads of grain to market, so they turned their harvest into a more portable product by distilling it into whiskey. The farmers believed the government's excise tax on distilled spirits was instituted to

1795 painting of Washington reviewing troops he would lead into battle against Pennsylvania farmers during the Whiskey Rebellion.

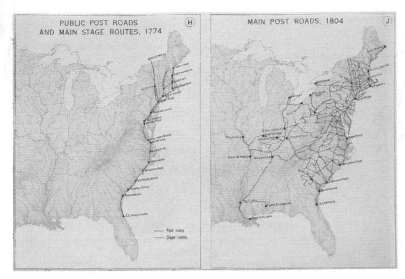

drive them out of the whiskey business for the benefit of large eastern distillers, and since they had few other sources of income, the tax was a serious issue for westerners. Luckily, the incoming Jefferson administration repealed the tax in 1801 and increasing Ohio River shipping provided new outlets for western produce.

Roads and Rivers

This map shows the growth of America's network of post roads between 1774 and 1804. On the eve of the Revolution, the only road that didn't hug the east coast followed the Hudson River Valley into upstate New York on its way to Montreal. This was one reason colonial Americans were so obsessed with the idea of trying to conquer Montreal and bring it into the United States. But less than thirty years later, riders working for the Post Office Department were carrying mail to nearly all the new settlements of the interior. The postal system's designer, Benjamin Franklin, understood that in order for the new Republic to function, information had to flow freely. Franklin set a low rate for newspapers, insuring that news would circulate widely in the newly settled areas. But it was one thing carrying saddlebags filled with letters and newspapers to the frontier, and something else moving people and freight.

1795 map of Pittsburgh, where the Allegheny and Monongahela Rivers join to form the Ohio River.

Rivers were the first important route to the interior of North America. The Ohio River, which begins at Pittsburgh and flows southwest to the Mississippi, helped people get to their new farms in the Ohio Valley and then helped them get their farm produce to market. The Ohio River Valley became one of the first areas of rapid settlement after the Revolution, along with the Mohawk River Valley in western New York. The importance of river shipping is illustrated by the fact that over fifty thousand miles of rivers and streams in the Mississippi watershed were used to float goods to the port of New Orleans. The dependence of western farmers on the Spanish port also explains why New Orleans was a strategic city for Americans in the War of 1812. Thomas Jefferson's 1803 purchase of the

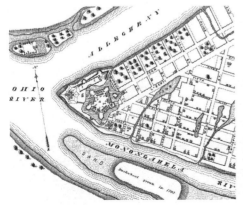

Louisiana Territory had actually begun as an attempt to buy the city of New Orleans, and Andrew Jackson's defense of the port during the War of 1812 was vital to insuring the success of western expansion.

Early westward expansion depended on rivers, and towns and cities built during this era were usually on a waterway. Pittsburgh, Columbus, Cincinnati, Louisville, St. Louis, Kansas City, Omaha, and St. Paul all owe their locations to the river systems they provide access to. Buffalo, Cleveland, Detroit, Chicago, and Milwaukee use the Great Lakes in the same way. These lakeside cities exploded after the Erie Canal opened a route from the Great Lakes to the Atlantic, and allowed New York to overtake New Orleans as the nation's most important commercial port. The 363-mile Erie Canal was so successful that another four thousand miles of canals were dug in America before the Civil War.

The Erie Canal, completed in 1825, connected the Great Lakes with the Hudson River, making New York City America's leading port.

In 1800, it took nearly two weeks to reach Buffalo from New York City, a month to get to Detroit, and six grueling weeks of travel to arrive at the swampy lakeshore settlement that would become Chicago. Thirty years later, Buffalo was just five days away, Detroit about ten days, and Chicago less than three weeks. Horses pulled canal boats from towpaths on shore, eliminating the strain of travel. And floating on calm water was infinitely more comfortable than spending weeks on a wagon or on horseback. The number of people willing to make long trips increased accordingly. The amount of freight shipped to New York, after the canal cut shipping costs by over ninety percent, increased astronomically. And goods flowed along the Canal in both directions, offering life-changing opportunities.

For example, within ten years of the Erie Canal's completion, the last fulling mill processing homespun cloth in Western New York shut its doors. Women no longer had to spin wool and weave their own textiles to make their family's clothing. They could buy bolts of wool and cotton fabrics from the merchant at the local general store who ground their family's grain into flour and shipped it on the Canal to eastern cities.

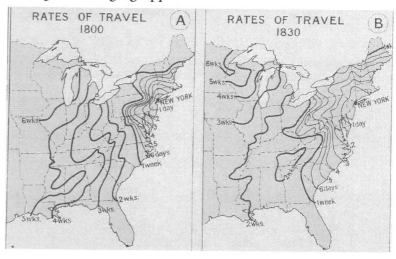

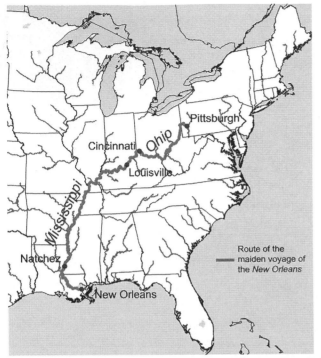

Route of the maiden voyage of the *New Orleans*

Steamboats

Steam power changed the nature of transportation. Until steam engines were put on boats, shipping had depended on either wind and river currents or on human and animal power. Goods easily floated south with river currents, but it was much more difficult and expensive to ship products against the currents to the frontier. Flatboats and rafts accumulated at downstream ports, and were often burned as firewood. Steam engines made it possible to sail upstream as easily and nearly as quickly as down, causing an explosion of travel and shipping that radically changed frontier life.

Steam engines were a product of early European industrialism. The first steam patent was granted to a Spanish inventor named Jerónimo Beaumont in 1606, whose engine drove a pump used to drain mines. Englishman James Watt's 1781 engine was the first to produce rotary power that could be used to drive mills, wheels, and propellers. Robert Fulton, an inventor who had previously patented a canal-dredging machine, visited Paris and caught steamboat fever. He sailed an experimental model on the Seine, and then returned home and launched the first commercial American steamboat on the Hudson River in 1807. The Clermont was able to sail upriver 150 miles from New York City to Albany in 32 hours. In 1811, Fulton built the New Orleans in Pittsburgh and began steamboat service on the Mississippi. Although Robert Fulton died a few years later of tuberculosis, his partners Nicholas Roosevelt and Robert Livingston carried on the business, and the age of riverboats was underway. The New Orleans was a large, heavy side-wheeler with a deep draft; it didn't take long for designers to settle on the familiar shallow-draft rear-paddle riverboats that carried freight on the Mississippi and its tributaries well into the 20th century. The shallower a riverboat's draft, the farther upriver it could go. Steam-powered riverboats soon pushed the transportation frontier to Fort Pierre in the Dakota territory and even to Fort Benton, Montana. Riverboats made it possible to ship goods in and out of nearly the whole area Thomas Jefferson had acquired in the Louisiana Purchase just a generation earlier. And steam-powered ocean shipping made the markets of Britain and Europe accessible to farmers and merchants in the middle of North America.

Railroads

The other transportation technology enabled by steam power was the railroad. But where steam-powered riverboats depended on rivers or occasionally on canals to run, a railroad could be built almost anywhere. Suddenly expansion wasn't limited by the routes nature had provided into the frontier.

1831 newspaper image of America's first steam locomotive, the Tom Thumb.

The first railroads were actually built on the East Coast before a steam engine was available to run them. Trains of cars were pulled by horses and looked a lot like stage-coaches on rails. But after Englishman George Stephenson's locomotives began pulling passengers and freight in northwestern England in the mid-1820s, Americans switched to steam. The first locomotive used to pull cars in America was the Tom Thumb, built in 1830 for the Baltimore and Ohio Railroad.

By 1850, over 9,000 miles of track had been laid, mostly connecting the northeast with western farmlands. The Mississippi was still the preferred route to market from Louisville and St. Louis south. But Cincinnati and Columbus were connected by rail to the Great Lake ports at Sandusky and Cleveland, giving the northern Ohio Valley fast access to New York markets. Detroit and Lake Michigan were also connected by rail, making the long steamboat trip around the northern end of Michigan's lower peninsula unnecessary.

By 1857, rail travelers could reach Chicago in less than two days, and could be almost anywhere in the northern Mississippi Valley in three. By 1860, on the eve of the Civil War, Chicago was already becoming the railroad hub of the Midwest. The Illinois Central Company had been chartered in 1851 to build a rail line from the lead mines of Galena to Cairo, where the Ohio and Mississippi Rivers joined. Galena is also located on the Mississippi on the northern border of Illinois, but the river's rapids north of St. Louis made transporting ore difficult, and illustrated the advantage of rails over rivers. A railroad line to Cairo, with a branch line to Chicago, would also attract settlers and investors to Illinois. Young Illinois attorney Abraham Lincoln helped the railroad lobby get the first federal land grant ever given to a railroad company. The company received 2.6 million acres

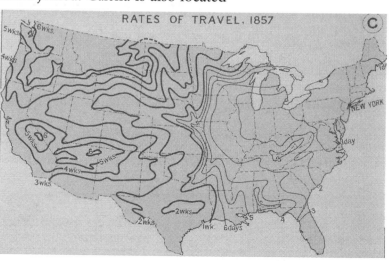

RATES OF TRAVEL, 1857

A. Lincoln, railroad lawyer, 1858.

1854 map of Illinois showing land granted to the Illinois Central.

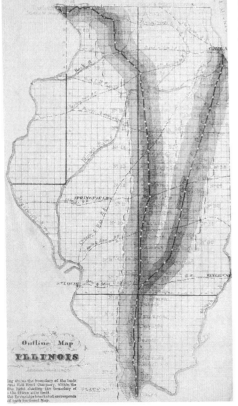

of land, and Illinois Senator Stephen Douglas helped design the checkerboard distribution of parcels that would become common for railroad land grants. The map below shows the extent of the land the government gave to the Illinois Central Company, which a few years later helped finance Lincoln's Presidential campaign against Douglas.

The North's advantage over the South in railroad miles and the Union Army's ability to move troops and supplies efficiently had a definite impact on the Civil War's outcome. In the years following the war, the shattered South added very little railroad track and repaired only a small portion of the tracks the Union Army had destroyed during the war, while rail miles in the North exploded. In 1869, the west coast was connected by rail, when the Union and Central Pacific Lines met at Promontory Point Utah on May 10th. The building of a transcontinental railroad was made possible by the Pacific Railroad Act, which President Lincoln had signed into law in 1862.

The Pacific Railroad Act was the first law allowing the federal government to give land directly to corporations. Previously the government had granted land to the states for the benefit of corporations. The Act granted ten square miles of land to the railroad companies for every mile of track they built. And land next to railroads always appreciated rapidly. This was a tremendous incentive to the railroad companies to lay just as much track as they could. Decisions to build lines were often based on the land granted, rather than on whether or not railroad companies expected the lines to carry enough traffic and generate enough freight revenue to pay for themselves. Between the Illinois Central grant of 1851 and the completion of the transcontinental line in 1869, the railroads received about 175 million acres of public land at no cost. This amounts to about seven percent of the land area of the contiguous 48 states, or an area slightly larger than Texas. For comparison, the Homestead Act distributed 246 million acres to American farmers between 1862 and 1934, but required homesteaders to live on and to farm the land continuously for five years or pay for their parcel. The justification for the residency requirement was that the government was concerned homesteaders would become speculators and flip their farms. Railroad land grants were made with no similar stipulations.

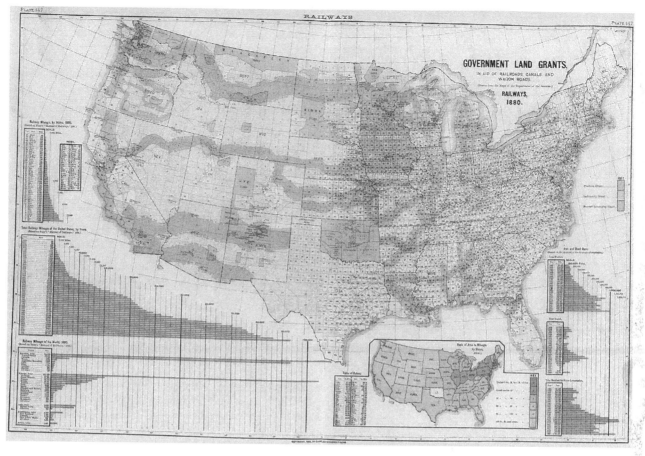

Railroad land grants exceeded the area of Texas. This map shows land grants up to 1880.

Public or Private?

It has often been argued that an infrastructure project as large as a transcontinental railway cannot be built without government assistance. The west coast and western territories needed to be brought into the Union, some historians have argued, and the only way to achieve this was with government-supported railroads. The same people who make this argument usually also claim that it would have been disastrous for the government to own the railroads it had made possible with its legislation, loans, and land grants. An undertaking of this scope and scale, they say, naturally requires that corporations be given monopolies and grants of natural resources and public credit. These arguments make it seem inevitable that giant corporations taking huge gifts from the public sector were necessary for America to move forward. History shows that this was not the only way a national rail system could have been built.

Although there are numerous examples of rail systems built and managed by the public sector in foreign countries, for the sake of sim-

George Custer, railroad employee. Note Northern Pacific stamp on the tent in this photo from Custer's 1874 mission providing security for railroad surveyors.

plicity I'll restrict my comparison to the United States. The Northern Pacific Railway, approved by Congress in 1864, built 6,800 miles of track to connect Lake Superior with Puget Sound. In return, the company was given 40 million acres of land in 50-mile checkerboards on either side of its tracks. Not only did the Northern Pacific rely on the government for land and financing, the railroad used the services of the U.S. Army to protect its surveyors and move Indians out of its way. When the Northern Pacific's proposed route cut through the center of the Great Sioux Reservation, established by the 1868 Fort Laramie Treaty, the corporation pressured the government to break the treaty. When George Custer announced that gold had been discovered in the Black Hills after an 1874 mission protecting Northern Pacific surveyors, Washington let the treaty be disregarded by the railroad and the prospectors. The Indians responded with the Great Sioux War of 1876, which culminated in the Battle of Little Big Horn, where Custer's Seventh Cavalry was wiped out by Sitting Bull and Crazy Horse, leading a force of Lakota, Cheyenne, and Arapaho warriors. But although the Indians won the battle, they lost the war. Less than a year later, the Sioux ceded the Black Hills to the United States in exchange for rations for the reservation.

In contrast, Canadian-American railroad entrepreneur James Jerome Hill built his Great Northern Railroad Line from St. Paul to Seattle during the last decades of the nineteenth century without causing a war and without receiving a single acre of free public land. The Great Northern bought land from the government for its right of way and to sell to settlers. Hill claimed proudly that his railway was built "without any government aid, even the right of way, through hundreds of miles of public lands, being paid for in cash." The Great Northern system connected the Northwest with a web of over 8,300 miles of track, and because Hill only built lines where traffic justified them, his was one of the few transcontinental railroad companies to avoid bankruptcy in the Panic of 1893.

J.J. Hill's Great Northern Railway in 1897. Hill boasted he had never taken government land grants or financial handouts to build his railroad.

Regardless of the ways they were financed and built, railroads, like the rivers before them, caused explosive growth. Chicago was a frontier village of 4,500 people in 1840. When Lincoln got the first land grant for the Illinois Central in 1851, the city's population was about 30,000. Twenty years later Chicago was the center of a growing railroad network, and had ten times the people. In 1880 the population was over 500,000, and ten years later Chicago held over a million people. We'll take a closer look at the changes railroads brought to Chicago in a Chapter Seven.

Internal Combustion

America's transportation revolution didn't end with steamboats and railroads. The development of the automobile ushered in a new era of personal mobility for Americans. Internal combustion engines were inexpensive to mass produce and much easier to operate than steam engines. Suddenly, around the turn of the twentieth century, it no longer took a huge capital investment and a team of engineers to buy and run motorized transportation. Even the workers on Henry Ford's assembly lines could aspire to owning their own Model Ts, especially after Ford doubled their wages to $5 a day.

Engineers had tried building smaller machines using steam engines, and there had been some successful steam-powered farm tractors, trucks, and even a few horseless carriages. But internal combustion engines delivered more power relative to their mass, allowing smaller machines to do more work. The first farm tractor was built by John Froehlich's small Waterloo Gasoline Traction Engine Company in 1892. Others began experimenting with internal combustion engines, and between 1907 and 1912 the number of tractors in American fields rose from 600 to 13,000. Eighty companies produced more than 20,000 tractors in 1913. The little Iowa company got off to a slow start and began building farm tractors in volume only after World War I. The Waterloo company was acquired by the John Deere Plow Company in 1918. Deere remains the world leader in self-propelled farm equipment.

The first internal combustion truck was built by Gottlieb Daimler in 1896, using an engine developed by Karl Benz the year before. World War I spurred innovation, and by the end of the war gasoline powered trucks had overtaken the steam truck market. Most large trucks now burn diesel fuel rather than gasoline, using a compression-ignition engine design patented by Rudolf Diesel in 1892.

Trucks and tractors, like cars, allowed people to go farther, carry more, and do more

work than had been possible using human and animal power. Trucking eventually challenged rail transport, especially after the development of semi-trailers and the Interstate Highway System, begun in 1956. Although the first truck engines only produced five to seven horsepower, they advanced quickly. Indiana mechanic Clessie Cummins built his first, six-horsepower diesel engine in 1919. Cummins is now a global corporation doing $20 billion in annual business, mostly in diesel engines. Their current heavy truck model is rated at 600 horsepower.

The Interstate Highway System was built by the federal government and is owned by the States.

The Open Road

It's easy to focus on the inventions and technological innovations of the internal combustion era and lose sight of the infrastructure that made these innovations valuable. But without paved roads to run on, there would have been fewer cars and trucks, and their impact on society and the environment would have been much different.

The biggest roadbuilding project in American history was the construction of the Interstate Highway System, which began with the Federal-Aid Highway Acts of 1944 and 1956. Unlike the transcontinental railroad project of the 1860s, the Interstate System was financed by the federal government and the roads are owned by the states. The system includes nearly 47,000 miles of highway, and the project was designed to be self-liquidating, so that the cost of the system did not contribute to the national debt. In addition to the Interstate System, American states, counties, cities and towns maintain a system of roads totalling nearly four million miles, about two thirds of which are paved.

Gasoline vs. Ethanol

The 1910 Ford Model T ran on either gasoline, kerosene, or ethanol. Over fifteen million were built, and their price dropped steadily from $800 in 1910 to $300 in 1925.

The tradeoff of internal combustion for the farmers and teamsters who first adopted it was that speed and power came at a price. Where horses and oxen were readily available in farm communities and cheap to maintain, tractors and trucks were an investment. And unlike horses and oxen, tractors and trucks needed to be fueled with petroleum that made them dependent on a faraway industry. This wasn't inevitable. Henry Ford and Charles Kettering, the chief engineer at General Motors, both believed that as engine compression ratios increased, their companies' engines would transition from gasoline to ethyl alcohol.

Although most history books repeat the story that Edwin Drake's famous 1858 oil strike in Titusville Pennsylvania came just as the world was running out of expensive whale oil, there was actually a thriving alcohol fuel market in the mid-nineteenth century. Ethanol was competitive with kerosene, and unlike kerosene was produced by many small distillers, creating competition that would continue to drive down prices. The ethanol industry was nearly destroyed when the Lincoln administration imposed a $2.08 per gallon tax on distilled alcohol between 1862 and 1864. A gallon of Standard Oil kerosene still cost only 58 cents, so kerosene took over the American fuel market.

1904 cartoon portraying Standard Oil as a giant octopus attacking industry and government.

But ethanol still had its advocates. The first American internal combustion engine, built in 1826 by Samuel Morey, had used grain alcohol because it was readily available. Nearly a century later, Henry Ford's Model T was designed to be convertible between kerosene, gasoline, and ethanol. General Motors chief engineer was convinced it was only a matter of time until ethanol was the fuel of choice.

So why aren't we all driving cars running

renewable fuels? Part of the answer, as you've probably already guessed, is that Standard Oil made the auto industry an offer they couldn't refuse. The oil company used its distribution network to make gasoline available everywhere it was needed, and made sure the price was so low that competitors could not profit if they entered the market. Standard Oil pioneered the practice of pricing below the cost of production to run competitors out of the business. The profits of the company's other divisions subsidized their short-term losses on gasoline. Predatory pricing was one of the main charges made against the company in the 1911 antitrust case that resulted in the breakup of the Standard Oil Trust.

Lead

Ethyl Corporation ad from the 1950s suggests that, like unicorns, corn (the source of ethanol) is just a funny old myth that shouldn't be taken too seriously.

But that's not the whole story. Using gasoline at high compression resulted in engine knocking. It was well-known that ethanol did not knock and Charles Kettering at General Motors had argued for years that the "most direct route which we now know for converting energy from its source, the sun, into a material suitable for use as a fuel is through vegetation to alcohol." Americans had been distilling alcohol fuels for generations.

Unfortunately, Charles Kettering worked for a corporation whose major shareholder was the Du Pont family, who also happened to own the biggest corporation in the chemical industry. It would be impossible for DuPont to profit or for General Motors to gain competitive advantage using alcohol fuels, since the distilling technology was universally available and the product was un-patentable. However, there was a profitable alternative.

Tetraethyl Lead (TEL) was a lubricating compound that could be added to gasoline to eliminate knocking. General Motors was granted a patent on its use as an anti-knock agent, and Standard Oil was granted a patent on its manufacture which was later extended to include DuPont. The companies founded Ethyl Corporation to market TEL and other fuel additives. Unfortunately, lead is a powerful neurotoxin, linked to learning disabilities and dementia. The federal government had misgivings about allowing lead additives, and in 1925 the Surgeon General temporarily suspended TEL's use and government scientists approached Ford engineers to quietly seek an alternative. In the 1930s, 19 federal bills and 31 state bills were introduced to promote alcohol use or blending. But the American Petroleum Industries Committee lobbied hard against them. Under industry pressure, the Federal Trade Commission even issued a restraining order forbidding commercial competitors from criticizing Ethyl gasoline as unsafe. By the mid-1930s, 90 percent of all gasoline contained TEL. Airborne lead pollution increased to over 625 times previous background levels, and when public concern continued to increase, the Ethyl Corporation was sold in 1962 in the largest leveraged buyout of its time. In the 1970s the newly-established Environmental Protection Agency finally took the stand other federal agencies had shied away from. The EPA declared emphatically that airborne lead posed a serious threat to public health, and the government forced automakers and the fuel industry to gradually eliminate the use of lead. TEL is now illegal in automotive gasoline, although it is still used in aviation and racing fuels.

Global Cargo

Two additional forms of transportation became increasingly important as the twentieth century ended. Commercial airplanes are only a little over a hundred years old; the first air cargo and airmail shipments were flown in 1910 and 1911. Air cargo was considered too expensive until express carriers like UPS and Federal Express revolutionized the shipping business in the 1990s. The global economy now measures air freight volumes in ton-miles. In 2014, the world shipped a little over 58 billion ton-miles of goods. Air freight also allows perishable items like fresh fruits and vegetables to be transported across oceans and continents from producers to consumers. This is a big business. Over 75 million tons of fresh produce are shipped annually, worth more than $50 billion.

For nonperishable items, container shipping has created a single global market. Standardized containers were invented by a trucker named Malcolm McLean, who realized it would save a lot of time and energy if his trucks didn't need to be loaded and unloaded at the port, but could just be hoisted on and off a cargo ship.

McLean refitted an oil tanker and made his first trip in 1956, carrying fifty-eight containers from Newark to Houston. Current annual shipping now exceeds 200 million semi-trailer sized containers. Containers can be shipped by sea, rail, truck, and even air, allowing just-in-time operators like Wal-Mart to manage a supply chain that relies much less on warehoused inventory, and more on product in transit.

But just as shifting from horse power to a gasoline truck or tractor a hundred years ago, shopping at Wal-Mart today introduces a new level of dependence. We are not only relying on high-tech transportation systems and the fuels they run on, but also on supply-chain software, international trade agreements and currency fluctuations, and even the political situations of faraway nations. As long as the costs of inputs like fuel and infrastructure like ports, highways, and open borders remains low, it's a great deal for the consumer and a source of immense profits to businesses and their shareholders. But a company like Wal-Mart is just as dependent on factors it can't control as its customers are. If any of these factors change, who will bear the cost?

Further Reading

Bill Kovarik, "Henry Ford, Charles Kettering and the Fuel of the Future," *Automotive History Review*, Spring, 1998. Available online at www.environmentalhistory.org

Marc Levinson, *The Box: How the Shipping Container Made the World Smaller and the World Economy Larger*, 2006.

Vaclav Smil, *Creating the Twentieth Century: Technical Innovations or 1867-1914 and their Lasting Impact*, 2005

George Rogers Taylor, *The Transportation Revolution, 1815-1860*, 1977.

Supplement: Reliving a past we can't remember

As I'm writing this chapter, gasoline prices are hovering just above $2 per gallon. A couple years ago, they were about double that. Petroleum industry analysts explain that this dramatic drop at the gas pump is due to overproduction by oil-producing nations who have dumped so much crude oil on the market that the price has dropped from about $100 per barrel in the summer of 2014 to about $45 in late 2015. Pundits warn that this glut is temporary and that prices will rise again. Some industry analysts worry that before they do rise, the low prices will destroy the shale oil and tar sands extraction industries they claim are vital to American energy independence. Others, convinced that tapping these sources does more harm than good, hope low prices will shut down fracking and tar pipelines. But they worry that the low prices making these techniques less attractive might also reduce the urgency of alternative energy initiatives such as wind and solar, and fuel options like ethanol.

The argument about energy independence, renewability, and ethanol isn't new: it has been going on for nearly a century. As mentioned in this chapter, Samuel Morey's 1826 internal combustion engine burned ethanol because it was readily available. Henry Ford and Charles Kettering both expected their future cars would burn alcohol fuels. Ford saw ethanol as a way to support American farmers and use grain surpluses that were depressing prices. Kettering's statement that alcohol was the best way to convert solar energy to fuel reflected a belief that it was better to live on annual solar "income" than to become dependent on drawing down fossil fuel "capital." And both men worried that dependence on gasoline would involve the United States in the affairs of faraway regions. A speaker at a 1936 conference sponsored by Ford remarked that the biggest known oil reserves were "in Persia…and in Russia. Do you think that is much defense for your children?"

Since energy is such an important and contentious issue today, why aren't we more aware that these debates are not new? General-purpose American History textbooks have a lot to cover, it's true. They can't go into detail on every issue. Checking the indexes of several popular textbooks reveals that if they address the petroleum industry at all, it's usually just to mention that Standard Oil pioneered horizontal business integration and that John D. Rockefeller eventually controlled 90% of the industry. But even respected histories of technology like Vaclav Smil's 2005 book, *Creating the Twentieth Century*, tell the story of early internal combustion as if gasoline was the only fuel used until the end of World War I, when diesel trucks began entering the market. In Smil's history, there was no solution to the "violent knocking that came with higher compression. That is why all pre-WWI engines worked with compression ratios no higher than 4.3-1 and why the ratio began to rise to modern levels (between 8 and 10) only after the introduction of leaded gasoline." This is simply not true, so why doesn't an expert like Smil know the facts?

As we've already seen, grain alcohol fuels were already widely used before the beginning of the kerosene and petroleum boom dominated by Standard Oil. Engineers at both Ford and General Motors were aware that ethanol ran at high compression ratios without knocking. So how is it possible that historians, even historians of technology, seem to be unaware of the battles fought in the early years of the twentieth century over what American drivers would put in their tanks?

Part of the answer, I think, is that the winners of those battles left more records for historians than the losers. History depends on evidence. A seemingly comprehensive history of the petroleum industry can be written, based on the mountains of documents in academic libraries and corporate archives. Books about companies like DuPont and Standard Oil, written by both supporters and opponents, could fill a library. Anyone who undertakes a new history of these subjects must read all this material, which leaves little time to dig for other perspectives.

The small local distillers of ethanol in the early twentieth century, unlike the corporations, left few documents. And finding the story of alcohol in the archives of Ford or General Motors requires dedication and persistence. A good percentage of the records left by these companies, after all, are not objective accounts at all. They're advertisements, public relations statements, and internal documents arguing not about what could be done, but about what they wanted to do.

As a result, the history we read tells the story of an apparently inevitable, unstoppable journey toward the petroleum-powered world we live in today. This type of history celebrates the winners while at the same time excusing them. When we assume the outcome was inevitable, we conclude that if it hadn't been Rockefeller, it would just have been somebody else. And that's the biggest problem. When we believe the present was inevitable, we lose the ability to imagine alternatives. In the past, and also in the present and the future.

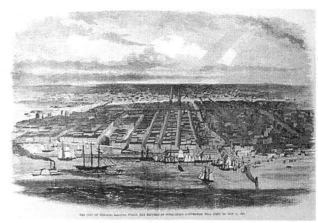

Chicago in 1860, on the eve of the Republican Convention that nominated Abraham Lincoln for the Presidency.

Chapter Seven: Centers and Peripheries

In this chapter we examine the complex relationships between Eastern and Western cities, as centers of production and consumption, and the peripheral places they depended on for raw materials and consumers.

Whenever people have achieved a surplus above mere subsistence, trade and the accumulation of resources have led to urbanization. Cities at the nodes of these trade networks have become centers of wealth, power, and culture. Artists and craftspeople often find patrons or markets for their work in cities, and government administrators and businesspeople often leave extensive records. So cities, both ancient and modern, are usually full of interesting information for historians.

But just because they offer so much information about the past, we shouldn't suppose that cities were the only places that mattered. Often historians interested in culture, or politics, or social movements focus too much attention on the cities where art was displayed, governments debated, or workers demonstrated. This narrow focus can distort our understanding of the past by suggesting that everything that happened in the city originated in the city. In fact, cities have always been centers for the accumulation, processing, and consumption of resources that come from the hinterlands around them.

As transportation improved, the hinterlands that were the sources of raw materials could be farther away. Grain from upstate New York farms could float down Erie Canal and Hudson River, cotton from Southern plantations could become cloth in Lowell mills, and silver mined in Potosí could become money in Europe. In each case, the cities in the center were just as dependent as they had ever been on their hinterlands, even though increasing distance might obscure the relationship. So it's important, as the distances widen and interactions become more complicated, to be careful we don't lose sight of the economic lifelines tying the centers with the peripheries.

In this chapter we'll consider the rise of new cities and new hinterlands as Americans pushed westward. The cities that developed on rivers, lakeshores, and railroad junctions benefited from the advances in transportation discussed previously. But the transportation would have been pointless and the cities empty without the surrounding rural areas that supplied food, fuel, and building materials. And the commodity agriculture, meat production, and forestry that developed alongside the cities likewise depended on urban businesses and populations who were the processors and consumers of their products.

Pork

Recall how difficult-to-ship grain west of the Appalachians was converted to whiskey by early Americans. This conversion was possible because there was more grain harvested than farm families needed to survive, and because rural people needed other things that it took cash to buy. Distilling whiskey not only made their surplus grain easier to transport, it increased its value per pound, and it added variety and interest that plain grain or flour lacked. In modern business terminology, the farmers diversified and added value.

A similar increase in variety and value happened when grain was fed to domesticated animals like poultry, cattle, and pigs. Even in primitive conditions, people prefer not to live by bread alone. In subsistence societies, these creatures foraged for themselves or ate waste products not fit for humans. In some societies, animals have continued to occupy this default livestock niche (some contemporary food activists argue we should move back toward this approach). But in America, when there was a surplus, even foods that could be eaten by people were often fed to livestock. These animals were a luxury for consumers and a living bank account for their owners. They stored the food energy of perishable surplus grain in

POLAND CHINA SOW, TEN MONTHS OLD.

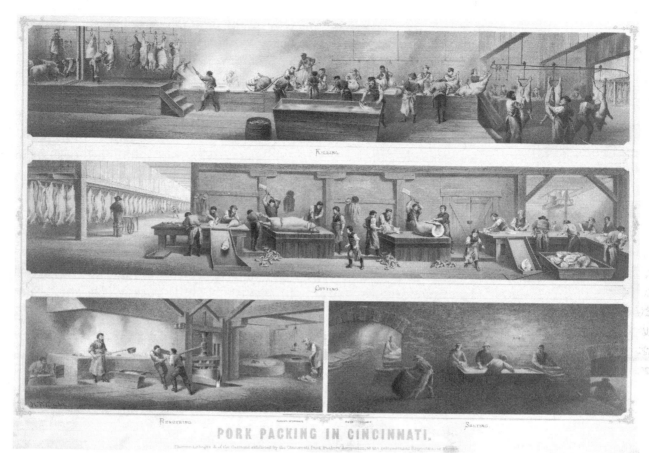

PORK PACKING IN CINCINNATI.

their flesh until there was a shortage, and then they were eaten. As time went on and surpluses became dependable, meat became a commodity that farmers could raise and sell for cash.

Pigs are extremely efficient converters of surplus grain to meat. They're omnivores that grow quickly and produce twice as much meat per pound of grain as sheep or cattle, which are ruminants and prefer grasses. A sow can be bred much earlier than a heifer, and will produce a litter of 6 to 12 piglets after four months gestation. Pigs were a favorite of homesteaders and frontier farmers because they would eat anything. Pigs could be turned loose to forage for acorns and were a great help to farmers rooting up tree stumps to clear fields. And pigs became the frontier's first big meat product for city markets because unlike beef, their flesh is easily preserved by smoking or salting.

In the early 1800s, Buffalo New York and Cincinnati Ohio became centers of pork processing. Bacon and hams were smoked, and pork was salted and packed in barrels for storage and shipping. The earliest packers were merchants in frontier towns like Chillicothe, Terre

Cincinnati, Ohio, 1841.

Haute, and Lafayette Indiana. As raising pigs for market became popular, farmers switched from the semi-wild razorback variety they'd brought to the frontier, and began raising premium foreign breeds like the Suffolk, Yorkshire, and Poland China. Popular farm periodicals like The Prairie Farmer were filled with articles on the merits of different breeds and how to crossbreed for improved results and hybrid vigor. Farmers became experts at calculating "the value of corn when sold in the form of pork," which required them to know not only feeding yields and feed prices, but also transportation costs and risks, and to have some idea of the demand for their product in faraway markets. And as specialized processors built larger businesses in the cities, they needed access to capital.

The operating costs of a pork processor were high. Fixed costs of production were low, especially compared to eastern industries like textiles that required large factories and expensive machinery to operate. But a county pork processor might buy 6,000 hogs to pack in a season, which in the mid-1840s cost about $45,000. A city packer processing 15,000 hogs would need over $100,000 of cash or credit. Packing quickly became big business. By the 1830s America replaced Ireland as Europe's source of cheap processed food. By the early 1840s, bacon and ham exports reached 166 million pounds. Shipments of processed pork were made easier by the growth of the rail network, but packers quickly realized that trains carrying barrels of salted pork could just as easily carry live animals. Railroads led to the concentration of packing in big cities like Cincinnati, Louisville, Chicago, and St. Louis. But even in the 1850s, when Cincinnati was known as Porkopolis and processed over a quarter million hogs a year, the big cities only accounted for 40 percent of the business. By 1877, the Midwest was processing 2,543,120 hogs a year. Year-round access to ice allowed what had once been a seasonal business to continue year-round. With the rise of ice-packing, some pork processors moved back to smaller cities. The big city packers took advantage of refrigerated shipping to branch out into beef.

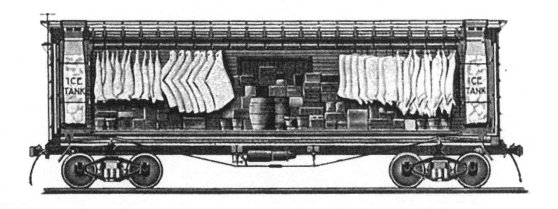

The Ice King

Frederic Tudor's ice-cutting operation, Spy Pond, Arlington Massachusetts, 1852.

One of America's forgotten industries that flourished during the nineteenth century was the ice business. Ice had always been important, but in early America it was a luxury product costing hundreds of dollars per ton. Ice was traditionally cut from ponds or lakes in the winter and stored in cellars or covered wells. In 1806, a 23-year old Harvard drop-out named Frederic Tudor bought a ship to carry a load of ice from his father's farm in Saugus Massachusetts to the Caribbean island, Martinique. After successfully delivering Massachusetts ice to Martinique, Tudor convinced the governments of Cuba and several other islands to grant him a monopoly on ice imports. By 1833, Tudor was shipping ice to Calcutta, India. After a four-month journey half-way around the world, his ship's cargo of 180 tons of New England ice had shrunk to only 100 tons, but Tudor still made a huge profit. Henry David Thoreau watched Tudor's workers cutting ice on Walden Pond, and remarked in his journal, "The sweltering inhabitants of Charleston and New Orleans, of Madras and Bombay and Calcutta, drink at my well." By 1865, two out of three homes in the Boston area had an icebox.

Like potash for soap and firewood for locomotive boilers, ice was something western settlers could quickly produce for eastern markets. Local entrepreneurs built icehouses near railroad lines and filled them from winter lakes. Midwestern pork packers like Gustavus Swift and Philip Armour saw an opportunity to expand their business. They were already shipping pork on ice, so why not ship chilled beef? Swift, Armour, and the other city packers contracted with icehouses along the lines, so their shipments were always cold. Refrigerated rail cars first carried dressed beef from Chicago to Eastern cities in the late 1850s. But local butchers resisted this invasion of their market, insisting that their freshly-killed local meat was tastier and safer. In 1878, Gustavus Swift developed the first practical ice-cooled refrigerated boxcar, or reefer. But adoption of the new technology was slow, and after ten years live cattle still outweighed dressed

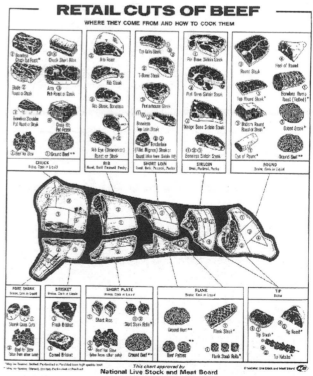

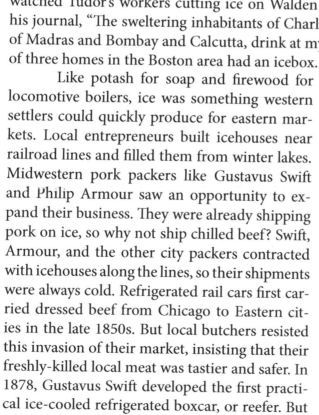

beef on the rails by four to one.

Because eastern butchers resisted the introduction of dressed beef and railroad companies didn't want to lose the revenue they earned shipping live cattle, corporations like Swift and Armour built their own fleets of reefer cars. By 1900 the packers owned over fifty thousand refrigerated freight cars and the old local butchers were overwhelmed. A few years later, a new generation of city butchers was forced by the government to give up slaughtering animals altogether and begin selling Chicago dressed beef.

Beef

Unlike pork, beef spoils rapidly when it's not refrigerated. The earliest solution to this problem was to ship live animals to market, where they'd be slaughtered and their meat processed for immediate sale by local butchers. Cattle-raising grew in the first half of the nineteenth century from something done on rangelands in California and Texas that were no good for crops, to a mainstream activity for Midwestern farmers. Cattle grow more slowly than pigs. But they are ruminants, which means they can eat not only the surplus grains farmers fed to pigs, but field grass, straw, and silage left over after wheat and corn was harvested.

Like pigs, cattle had been on the frontier from the earliest days. Milk cows were common on family farms, and oxen (neutered bulls) were preferred over horses as draft animals, due to their strength and endurance. When either of these animals came to the end of its productive farm life, they were slaughtered and eaten.

In the city, of course, there was less room for a family milk-cow. Although it was actually common in many cities for poor people to keep pigs that foraged the neighborhoods, urban cattle required large amounts of hay and had to be looked af-

ter. Many city-dwellers relied on dairymen for their milk and on their local butchers to kill and process their steaks and roasts. Herds of cattle were often walked across the plains in long cattle drives to a railhead where they would be loaded onto freight cars for shipment to distant cities. These animals might walk hundreds of miles from their rangelands to the railhead, resulting in tremendous weight loss. Arriving at their destinations, they would have to be finished: fed for a while to regain their weight. And when they were processed by a local butcher, up to 60% of the animals' mass would still have to be discarded as inedible waste.

Chicago beef packers saw an opportunity. Finishing and processing live animals shipped to eastern cities added to beef's cost. And local butchers often threw away parts of the carcass that could be rendered into marketable products, especially if they could be processed in large volume.

But dressed beef was highly perishable, and had to be sold quickly after processing. In spite of their fleets of reefer cars, corporations like Swift and Armour were often forced to sell dressed beef below its cost of production, in order to move the product before it went bad. The big meat packers turned this liability into an asset, buying the urban market with low prices and using the profits from other product lines to subsidize their losses. Prices for Chicago dressed beef were slashed to the point butchers couldn't match them with fresh meat. Eastern city customers naturally wanted the biggest cut they could get for their dollar, and the Chicago packers made sure it was theirs. Swift's instructions to his salesmen were, "If you're going to lose money, lose it. But don't let 'em nose you out."

Cattle pens at Chicago's Union Stock Yard, 1909.

The Jungle

Chicago's famous Union Stock Yards were opened in 1864, on 320 acres of swampy land southwest of the city. Animal pens were connected to the railroads with fifteen miles of track. The Yards processed two million animals in 1870, and by 1890 they were processing 9 million animals a year. By 1900, after an expansion, the 475-acre stockyard employed 25,000 people and produced over 80 percent of the meat sold in America. The Yards contained nearly 2,500 livestock pens which could house 75,000 hogs, 21,000 cattle, and 22,000 sheep at a time. The Yards used 500,000 gallons of water daily and

THE LODGER AND CHICAGO TINNED MEAT

CORNED BEEF CHICAGO

THE LODGER HAS A FIT AND IS
SUPPORTED BY THE LANDLADY

A postcard from a popular series printed in England in 1907, satirizing Chicago Tinned Meat.

pumped the waste into the South Fork of the Chicago River in an area that became known as Bubbly Creek. According to Chicago tradition, the creek still bubbles, nearly a hundred years later.

Growth of the Chicago meat packing industry was resisted by butchers, distrusted by consumers, and criticized by labor activists. Most Americans at the beginning of the twentieth century lived on farms or in small towns, and valued the face-to-face relationships that were still a big part of their commercial lives. And accounts of the Chicago meat packing industry were shocking. Upton Sinclair's 1906 novel, *The Jungle*, depicted the stockyards and packing plants as inhumane, unsanitary, and run by corrupt businessmen who cut corners and victimized their immigrant workers. In a widely-read endorsement of *The Jungle*, famous author Jack London called it "the Uncle Tom's Cabin of wage slavery."

Although President Theodore Roosevelt was suspicious of Sinclair and considered him a dangerous socialist, he commissioned an investigation that quickly confirmed Sinclair's sensational claims. The government report led directly to the Federal Meat Inspection Act of 1906, designed to ensure that meat products used as food were processed under sanitary conditions and were correctly labeled. This type of regulation had never been needed when Americans slaughtered and processed their own farm animals or bought their meat from local butchers who they knew and trusted.

Small local companies lived and died by their reputations in a way large, remote corporations did not. Government regulation was considered crucial to enforcing safety and quality controls in the stockyards and packing plants of Chicago because it was impossible for consumers to make corporations accountable the way they could their local butcher. What had once been a face-to-face, personal interaction between a merchant and the small community he was a part of had become a faceless transaction in a national market. The personal accountability that was part of face-to-face local commerce disappeared. Consumers were scattered and hard to organize, while producers were few and powerful. Ironically, although businessmen like Swift and Armour may initially have been offended by what they considered government intrusion into their operations, regulation saved their businesses by creating consumer trust in their processed meats, especially after people had read *The Jungle*.

The Meat Inspection Act and the Pure Food and Drug Act that

followed it made State Governments responsible for inspecting meat sold inside their borders, and made the Federal Government responsible for meat sold across state borders or exported. The USDA also provided meat grading (Prime, Choice, and Select) as an optional service for a fee. But health and safety inspections were mandatory and were paid for by the government.

USDA meat inspectors on the Swift hog line, 1906.

Although meat packers such as Armour and Swift may not have welcomed inspectors, corporations actually received a valuable government service at taxpayer expense. USDA inspections cost the meat packers nothing, calmed the suspicions of consumers, and restored trust in the corporate brands. Local butchers, who had never needed government inspectors to convince customers that their shops were clean or their meat safe, found themselves at an extreme disadvantage after government inspectors began stamping sides of Chicago beef with dye stamps declaring the meat wholesome. When the new laws went a step further and declared butchers couldn't sell un-inspected meat at all, and there weren't enough USDA inspectors to visit every local slaughterhouse and butcher shop and certify them, local operators were forced to resell Chicago meat or go of business. Criticized for interfering in free enterprise, the government had actually wiped out the Chicago meat industry's competition through regulation.

There are still a few local meat processors scattered about the Midwest. We call them lockers, and they exist because some farmers still raise a few animals for their own family use, and because Midwesterners hunt deer. Lockers and their customers are not allowed to sell meat without USDA inspection, but the lockers can process uninspected carcasses for a fee. Every package of meat cut for home use at a locker must be marked with a stamp reading NFS: Not for Sale.

As a result of USDA regulations implemented a century ago, it is very difficult for local entrepreneurs to return to the business model of the pre-*Jungle* era when customers knew their merchants and producers lived and died by their personal integrity and the quality of their product. Localvores and libertarians such as Virginia farmer-author Joel Salatin have criticized today's regulatory regime, claiming it protects global food corporations from competition by small producers. Critics of the current system suggest the global concentration of meat processing has gone too far, but the trend shows no signs of stopping. America's largest pork pack-

er, Smithfield Foods, was recently purchased by the Shuanghui Group of China for nearly $5 billion.

Lumber & Modern Homes

In addition to processing rural foods for national markets, urban industries depended on raw materials from their hinterlands. Eastern cites grew around industries like the textile mills along the Merrimack River, processing cotton from Southern plantations. Western cities surrounded by undeveloped country became conduits for the natural resources of the frontier. In addition to meat-packing, Chicago became a center of the lumber industry.

Cutting trees in frontier forests was a winter activity, beginning each November after the harvest. Winter logging camps filled with Midwestern farmers or their sons, eager to supplement the season's farm produce with some cash earnings. Another reason logging was a winter activity was because it was difficult to get white pine out of the woods at any other time. Pine forests were often boggy, and sixteen-foot sections of tree trunk were easier to slide over frozen roads. Lumbermen stacked the logs on horse-drawn sleds they drove over iced logging trails. Logs were piled beside frozen streams throughout the winter, waiting for the spring snowmelt that would carry the timber downstream to Lake Michigan. Most of the timber that made its way to Chicago was floated across the lake. Timber came from Michigan, Wisconsin, and as far away as Minnesota. In 1879, *The Lumberman* magazine reported that "There is not today a navigable creek in the state of Michigan or Wisconsin [or] Minnesota, upon whose banks, to the head waters, the better grade of timber is still standing within a distance of two

70,000 Sears Modern Homes like this 1921 Colonial were shipped by rail to customers all over America.

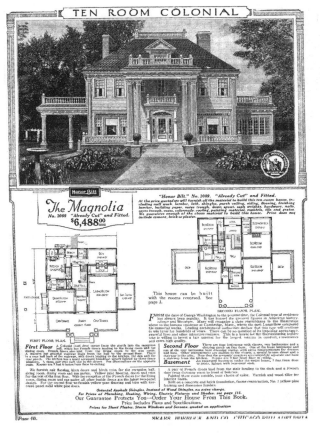

to three miles."

One of the major markets for Midwestern lumber processed in Chicago was housebuilding. Dimensional softwood lumber of the kind we're familiar with today made a new style of construction possible. Instead of hardwood-framed, post and beam construction requiring special skills, balloon-framing allowed houses to be built by relatively unskilled carpenters. Early American houses had been built of local hardwoods and had often been constructed in community efforts like the barn-raisings still held in traditionalist communities. Balloon houses were so easy to build that shoppers could buy them from mail order catalogs. In 1908, Chicago-based Sears Roebuck Company published its first *Book of Modern Homes and Building Plans*, which included 44 designs ranging in price from $360 to $2,890. Sears rail-shipped more than 70,000 catalog home kits between 1908 and 1940, in 370 designs. The ready-to-build kits included everything but concrete and bricks for their foundations. Competing regional and national companies sprang up, and the balloon construction style quickly became universal among American house-builders.

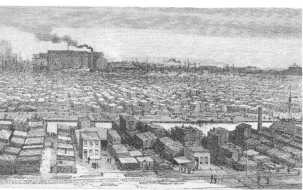

Chicago lumber district depicted in Harpers Weekly Magazine, 1883.

Fire

Lumber production in the Great Lakes region peaked in the early 1890s and then fell sharply when the industry moved to the Pacific Northwest. The cutover area covered several states, and the forest was usually clear cut. While removal of the Midwest's forests created potential new farmlands, the debris left by the cutover first needed to be cleared. Clearing the branches and debris left when pine forests were cut was often accomplished with fire, leading to some of the worst forest fires in American history. But sometimes the environmental impact on remote, resource-producing hinterlands is harder to see than the growth and profit being generated in the processing cities. Contemporary media and history often celebrate the achievements of innovators and entrepreneurs in the centers, without counting the costs to environments, communities, and people on the peripheries.

The Peshtigo Fire, October 8, 1871, killed 1,500 people in a town of 1,700 and destroyed 2,400 square miles of forest.

Our failure to charge these peripheral costs against the value created at the center happens so frequently that, as I've mentioned in earlier chapters, economists coined the term externality to describe it.

For example, while the Great Chicago Fire of 1871 was making national news, a much larger blaze two days earlier that had completely destroyed Peshtigo, Wisconsin was not. The Peshtigo fire, a direct result of the cutover, killed fifteen hundred people in the small town, five times the number killed in Chicago. But unlike Chicago's fire, the Peshtigo disaster was mostly ignored at the time, and has been virtually forgotten by historians outside Wisconsin.

Similar disasters in the cutover region included the Great Michigan fire of 1881, when over a million acres burned, the Hinckley, Minnesota fire of 1894, and the Cloquet, Minnesota fire of 1918. The deaths and destruction caused by these fires were a tangible cost of Chicago's timber industry. But they were faraway and external to the calculation of Chicago lumber companies' profits. The fires were a cost of doing business, but the cost was socialized while the profits were privatized. In a final irony, to the disappointment of would-be farmers, the boosters who advertised the cutover as a promising new agricultural region were wrong. Cutover pine-forest soils turned out to be thin and easily eroded in floods that became frequent once there were no live tree roots left to hold the soil and absorb rainfall.

Flour

The flour-milling district of Minneapolis, at St. Anthony Falls on the Mississippi River, 1893.

Chicago wasn't the only Midwestern city that depended on resource-rich hinterlands for its growth. During the early decades of American history, as we've seen, farmers grew wheat for home use and milled it at local grist mills. Surplus flour was packed in barrels by merchant millers and shipped to eastern markets. But as railroads made western farmlands more accessible, urban merchants built mills of their own and began buying unprocessed grain directly from farmers.

The creation of global markets, the building of national consumer brands, and the reduction of the farmer to a mere raw material supplier all happened about the same time, in the flour-milling business. Chicago was one center of this consolidation. Another was Minneapolis, home of the familiar brands Pillsbury and

General Mills, whose Gold Medal Flour can still be seen on supermarket shelves across America.

When farmers milled their grain locally and sold it close to home, people were able to buy flour from producers they trusted. The quality of the farmer's wheat and the care the miller took processing it into flour mattered. Even factors such as a farmer's reputation in the community or whether he paid his debts on time could influence a customer's buying decision. Consumers bought from people they knew, and often from people they had long-term relationships with. Farmers were also able to take advantage of long-term local relationships when it was time to sell their harvests. Producers had a bit more leverage, when they could negotiate with their miller face to face.

Personal accountability and face-to-face relationships were swept away when farmers began carting their grain to elevators by the railroad for shipment to big-city flour mills. The bulk elevator was an innovation developed in another mill city, Buffalo, in the late 1820s after the opening of the Erie Canal. Elevators allowed large quantities of grain to be handled rapidly and stored together. Wheat might still be hauled to the elevator by individual farmers in bags with the farmer's name on it. But as soon as it was unloaded the grain went into bulk storage bins where it was mixed with everyone else's grain. A particular farmer's special attention to his fields, or to timing his harvest and drying and threshing his grain carefully, was lost along with his identity. Everyone's grain went into the

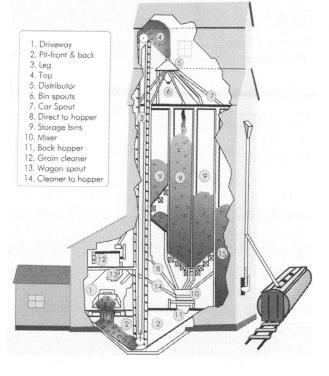

Diagram of a grain elevator. Note bulk storage bins.

1. Driveway
2. Pit-front & back
3. Leg
4. Top
5. Distributor
6. Bin spouts
7. Car Spout
8. Direct to hopper
9. Storage bins
10. Mixer
11. Back hopper
12. Grain cleaner
13. Wagon spout
14. Cleaner to hopper

same railroad cars and when the train arrived in Minneapolis, it didn't even really matter where it had come from. Trains from all across the Midwest converged on Minneapolis because its millers had developed a new technology called the rolling mill, and in the last decades of the nineteenth century the Mill City became the world leader in flour production.

When Minnesota became the 32nd state in 1858, the population of Minneapolis was only about five thousand. The town had grown up around the Falls of St. Anthony, where the water power of the first major falls on the Mississippi River was used to saw lumber and grind flour. By 1870, there were about 13,000 people in the growing city and large-scale flour mills had taken over the river in much the same way textile corporations had taken over eastern rivers. Twenty years later, when the flour-milling industry reached its peak, Minneapolis had grown to over 165,000 and the Mississippi was lined with corporate mills, connected by a dedicated railroad bridge crossing between them.

Less Corn, More Hell

Populist orator Mary Elizabeth Lease (1850-1933) told farmers they should organize and "Raise less corn and more hell."

Grain production surged as farmers devoted more acres to easy-to-sell cash crops. As supply increased, the price farmers got for a bushel of wheat fell from $1.06 in 1870 to $.63 in 1897, and corn dropped from $.43 to $.30. Farmers understood they were overproducing, but they also believed the game was rigged against them. Countless small farmers sold their grain to a few big corporations, and the farmers were charged higher freight rates than the railroads' favored corporate customers.

To make matters worse, when farmers entered the market to buy equipment, they once again felt they were on the wrong end of a system that pitted wealthy city corporations against powerless rural folk. In 1902 Wall Street financier J. P. Morgan merged the McCormick Harvesting Machine Company, the Deering Harvester Company, and three smaller farm machine companies into the International Harvester Company. After the biggest merger of its time, the farm equipment market consisted of 29 million farmers (38 percent of the American population), but only one $120 million corporation they could buy harvesters from.

Economic imbalance between businesses in the center and farmers at the periphery led to political mobilization. Farmers joined groups like the National Grange, began cooperatives to sell their produce and buy equipment and supplies, and helped create the Populist movement. The People's Party never won a Presidential election, although their candidate, William Jennings Bryan, served as Secretary of State to Woodrow Wilson. But they elected several Midwestern Governors and dozens of

Farmers resented a government "of the monopolists, by the monopolists, for the monopolists," as the caption of this 1889 cartoon read.

Congressmen. Populists were key to the passage of the Sherman Antitrust Act and to its application against monopolies. In 1914, following the breakup of Standard Oil, International Harvester became the next major target of an antitrust suit (it survived).

The pattern of urban processing centers depending on resource-producing hinterlands repeated as Americans moved westward. This wasn't the only way growth could have happened in America. It was the result of legal, political, and cultural choices. Enabled by transportation and encouraged by demand from urban consumers, products like meat, lumber, and flour that had once been produced locally and used by customers who knew the producers, became standardized commodities in national markets. As these markets expanded, big companies benefitted from their access to capital and their ability to create brands like Sears Modern Homes, Swift Premium Bacon, and Gold Medal Flour. But another, sometimes hidden factor in this change was the government's role in subsidizing these central processors by ensuring product safety and establishing standards of quality. And the effectiveness of concentrated economic power when it's pitted against small, disorganized opponents should not be underestimated.

Recognizing how quickly we changed from a society of farmers and small-town people doing business with neighbors, to an impersonal market where billions of consumers buy from a few immense corporations is crucial to understanding the present. The centers are now global, and the periphery includes most Americans. New technology and new markets helped the American West grow, and led to our society of pre-fabricated homes and processed foods. But in the long run, the centers accumulated more economic and political power than the periphery. City corporations gained the upper hand, partly by business and technical innovation, but partly by ignoring external costs at the periphery and taking advantage of government subsidies. That is, economic and political power helped some people benefit more than others from this change. The point is not that change shouldn't have happened, but that if we understand what actually happened, we may be better equipped to consider where we go from here.

Further Reading:

William Cronon, *Nature's Metropolis: Chicago and the Great West*. 1991.

Charles Postel, *The Populist Vision*. 2007.

Joel Salatin, *Folks, This Ain't Normal: A Farmer's Advice for Happier Hens, Healthier People, and a Better World*. 2011.

Upton Sinclair, *The Jungle*. 1906.

Supplement: Getting past theory

William Cronon's second book, *Nature's Metropolis,* uses the history of Chicago to illustrate the complex relationships between the city and the countryside in American history. Beginning and ending with a personal memory of a childhood journey from New England to Wisconsin that took him through Chicago, Cronon concludes "We fool ourselves if we think we can choose between [country and city], for the green lake and the orange cloud are creatures of the same landscape" (385). The text is a series of increasingly fine-grained illustrations of this point.

Cronon uses several interpretive theories to explore Chicago's history, and he points out some of their limitations. Frederick Jackson Turner's idea that the frontier "recapitulated the social evolution of human civilization" and provided the "source of American energy, individualism, and political democracy" (31) fails to account for the rapid, booster-driven growth of Chicago as an urban center. Turner didn't give enough credit, Cronon says, to the market as an agent of both rural and urban change. "Urban-rural commerce," he says, "was the motor of frontier change, a fact that the boosters understood better than Turner" (48).

Cronon uses Johann Heinrich von Thünen's Isolated State theory and more recent Central Place theory to correct Turner's perspective. Von Thünen's idealized economy creates a series of concentric rings drawn primarily on the basis of transportation costs. While acknowledging the heavy qualifications necessary to apply this model in the real world, Cronon says it fits Chicago. By focusing attention on the growth of rail transport, which not only lowered costs but more importantly eliminated risk and smoothed seasonality, the theory explains some of the features of Chicago's western "hinterland." But, as Cronon says, both theories are "profoundly static and ahistorical." Worse, like Turner, a model in which Chicago gradually emerges as an Isolated State is simply untrue. "Far from being a gradual, bottom-up process...nearly the opposite was true," Cronon says. "The highest-ranking regional metropolis consolidated its role at a very early date, and promoted the communities in its hinterland as much as they promoted it" (282). Since the West is the result of symbiotic, simultaneous growth of city and country, Cronon says, neither can claim historic precedence. The agrarian arguments of Thomas Jefferson and Andrew Jackson don't apply; at least not in the straightforward ways their proponents had hoped they would.

As readers familiar with Cronon would expect, he is always quick to point out ecological and historical backgrounds ignored by others. The western frontier was not "free" as Turner said, Cronon reminds. It was taken in conquest from the previous residents. Nor was it pristine. Western prairies were the product of Indian burning and hunting practices, as demonstrated by the incursion of oak and hemlock on ranches and homesteads once whites suppressed fire. Similarly, Cronon regularly begins descriptions of regions like Wisconsin timberlands or western rangelands with surveys of their ecological histories going back to the ice age. This nod to big history not only helps reinforce the ecological underpinning of Cronon's argument, it serves as an antidote to the alienation Cronon says is produced by separating economic production from consumption.

Chicago, says Cronon, cannot attribute its rapid growth in the last third of the nineteenth century simply to being a central place. Chicago is a central place now (of a much smaller hinterland than it possessed in its heyday), but it grew as a gateway. Beginning with a description of the many ways Chicago stood at the boundaries of ecosystems, continental watersheds, glacial termini, rural and urban society, railroad "trunk and fan" (90), and "natural and cultural landscapes" (25), Cronon shows Chicago grew by bridging the gap between the east (primarily New York) and the west (all the way to the Rockies). In Chicago, eastern capital met western raw materials and consumers. Railroads, finance, and information gave Chicago temporary advantages. Boosterism, the Civil War, and momentum added to Chicago's lead, which the city held until newer technologies, population changes, and the problems of success ended its predominance.

Along the way, Cronon tells fascinating stories about the standardization of timekeeping, the growth of organization and capitalism in the railroads, the abstraction of commodities into futures, the conversion of food production into industry, and the creation of the familiar consumer world. Each successive story highlights the market's increasing and ironic tendency to "obscure the connections between Chicago's trade and its earthly roots (264)." The "geography of capital," Cronon says, "produced a landscape of obscured connections" (340). But he doesn't really explain the process behind this progressive separation of producers from consumers, so it's unclear whether it is unique to Chicago or a symptom of a more universal alienation.

Agrarian resistance is mentioned primarily in the context of the Granger Laws, with a few suggestive references to Chicago-published papers like *The Prairie Farmer*. The most important feature of *Nature's Metropolis* is Cronon's story of the actual historical development of the Midwest as a single, interdependent process. While earlier Eastern settlement may have followed a different path, the growth of the Midwest as a single unit is crucially important if we are going to understand the politics of rural urban relations in the Populist and Progressive eras.

Chapter Eight: Green Revolution

Although we may not be aware of it, the continued existence of the modern world depends on three minerals. In this chapter we'll explore the history of fertilizer.

In the last few chapters, we've watched Americans spread across the continent. From the original thirteen colonies, the history of the United States seems to be a straightforward story of westward expansion. Beginning with the colonists' resistance to the Crown's restrictive Proclamation, Americans took advantage of the opportunities provided by the Northwest Ordinance, the Louisiana Purchase, the Mexican-American War, and the Oregon Treaty, to seek their fortunes on the frontier. Expansion was achieved partly by hardworking farmers, ranchers, and miners on the countryside, and partly by urban wage-workers and businesses in new western cities. These pioneers were aided by capital from eastern and overseas financial markets, by improving transportation networks, and by eastern city workers and capitalists who processed and consumed the products of fields, forests, and mines.

But not all the significant movement in American History was east to west. The growth of eastern cities depended on resources acquired on the frontier, so the flow of raw materials like farm products, timber, and minerals (which we'll examine in Chapter Twelve) from west to east was vitally important to the nation's growth. Manifest Destiny was as much about securing access to these resources as it was about planting the stars and stripes from sea to shining sea. And sometimes, important changes actually originated in the west, and expanded eastward.

The expansion and growth of both the West and the East depended on the ability of farmers to continue producing food for growing populations and for export. The biggest single factor in the continuing farm bonanza was soil fertility. In the 1840s, German chemist Justus von Liebig discovered that the chemicals nitrogen, phosphorus, and potassium were essential to plant growth. Farm soils naturally lose fertility unless fields are given time to regenerate between crop plantings or amendments are added. Liebig announced that instead of leaving fields fallow for years between crop plantings, farmers could amend the soil with the chemicals plants needed. We'll examine each of these chemicals, beginning with the element often considered the most important soil amendment, nitrogen. During the crucial period when America's commercial farmers became responsible for feeding the growing nation, nitrogen came from the west.

Green Manure

When settlers cut and burned forests to build farms, the thin soils of the forest floors got an initial productivity boost from leaf mulch and from the ashes of burned trees. This fertility was used up in a few years, unless the farmer rotated crops and pasture, or added manure to the soil. The prairie soils settlers found farther west were deeper and more fertile than eastern forest soils. Tall-grass prairies grew from the Canadian border to Texas, and as the name suggests, some of the grasses grew six to nine feet tall. When Laura Ingalls's parents told her not to stray too far onto the prairie in the Little House books, it was because they were afraid of losing her in the tall grass.

The Great Plains consists of (from west to east) short-grass, mixed-grass, and tall-grass prairies.

In addition to being tall, the prairies were deep. After millennia of growth and decay, prairie vegetation had left a layer of humus ten feet deep. The roots of perennial grasses took advantage of this depth, drawing water and nutrients from well below the surface. When settlers came with their John Deere

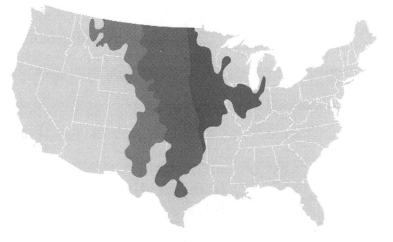

Alfalfa, known in the 1800s as Lucerne or Chili Clover, from an 1891 botanical.

cast steel plows, they only turned the top foot or so of this organic layer. But even so, the prairie offered some of the richest soils American settlers had ever seen, and western farmers wrote their families and friends back east boasting of the land and the great yields they got farming it.

In the long run, even the most fertile soils will be depleted after years of growing annual crops that don't return any nutrients. Smaller farms were able to spread manure from livestock, but as their fields grew from a few acres to a few hundred, most farmers found there wasn't enough manure to spread. Commercial farmers, who specialized in growing wheat or corn for the market, began planting fields with the cash crops every year, rather than rotating grain planting with fallow planting and grazing animals that would return at least some manure to the pasture. A new source of fertility was needed to prevent the agricultural balloon from deflating.

In addition to spreading manure, it has long been known that planting legumes is an effective method of returning nitrogen to the soil. Although nitrogen is the most common element in Earth's atmosphere, atmospheric nitrogen is very stable and unreactive. Plants can't use nitrogen until it's converted to nitrogen oxides, nitrates, or ammonia. Legumes have evolved a symbiotic relationship with Rhizobium bacteria, which live in nodules on the plants' roots and break the bonds of atmospheric nitrogen. When legumes are grown on a field and then plowed under, the nitrogen becomes available for the next crop. One of the most effective legume crops used as a green manure is alfalfa.

Alfalfa is native to Eurasia, where Siberian horse tribes began feeding it to their animals over three thousand years ago. Cortés and Pizarro brought alfalfa to Mexico and Peru in the early 1500s, and it quickly spread to across Central and South America. When North American colonists planted alfalfa, which they called lucerne, the plant did poorly in the cool, acidic soils of the Atlantic colonies. But a Chilean miner brought alfalfa to California during the Gold Rush. The climates of Chile and California are nearly identical, and "Chili Clover" thrived in western pastures, renewing the soil and providing ten times the nutrition of regular grasses for the growing dairy herds of California. In the early 1850s, the U.S. Patent Office mailed out thousands of packets of alfalfa seed to farmers across the country. Alfalfa swept eastward from California, jumping quickly to Utah, Colorado, Kansas, and Nebraska. Today, the Chilean import is so common in American fields, almost no one remembers it's not a native species.

Guano

The first commercial fertilizers were made from guano, the droppings of seabirds living on islands off the western shores of South America. Guano comes from the Quechua Indian word *Wanu*, which means any excrement used as a soil additive in farming. Natives of the Andes have been mining guano on the coast and islands for at least 1,500 years, according to archaeologists. Spanish colonial records noted that Inca rulers considered protecting the cormorants that were the main source of guano so important, they made disturbing the birds' nesting areas a capital offense. Guano was carried from the coast up into the Andes on the backs of llamas, for use on the terraced farms surrounding highland cities like Machu Picchu.

Workers mining guano on a Peruvian island, 1860.

Although surrounded by ocean, the islands off the western coast of South America are arid. Like the deserts they face on the mainland, some experience no rain at all. Seabirds such as cormorants and pelicans have lived on these islands by the millions, for thousands of years. Over that time, they've left literal mountains of droppings, which due to the lack of rain have simply piled up. The guano contains 8 to 16 percent nitrogen, 8 to 12 percent phosphorus, and 2 to 3 percent potassium, which makes it an excellent fertilizer without any mixing. It just needs to be chopped off the mountain, ground up, and spread on fields.

Prussian explorer Alexander von Humboldt visited the guano islands around 1802, and publicized guano's value as a fertilizer throughout Europe. Seeing a lucrative business opportunity, Europeans and Americans fell on the area in a guano rush, and by the middle of the century several nations had enlisted the work of Chinese peasants in a Pacific labor system that has been compared with the slavery of the Atlantic world. Although the Chinese workers were technically free, they were often tricked into labor contracts promising work in California. Once they reached the guano islands, there was no way off. Over a hundred thousand Chinese workers were imported to the islands in the second half of the nineteenth century.

Guano was so profitable that the U.S. Congress passed a Guano Islands Act in 1856. The law provided incentives for American sailors to find and claim undefended islands for America by giving the discoverer exclusive rights to the guano discovered. Islands claimed under the Act include parts of the Hawaiian chain, Midway Atoll, part of American Samoa, and several islands still disputed with Colombia.

The guano islands were so valuable that two wars were fought over them. Chile and Peru fought Spain in the Chincha Islands War, 1864-66, and defeated the Spanish Empire. Once Spain's claim had been successfully challenged, Chile took many of the guano islands from Peru, along with the nitrate fields of the Atacama Desert, in the War of the Pacific, 1879-83.

Nitrate

After about 1870, guano was overtaken as a source of nitrogen by desert soils called Caliche. These soils were located in the Atacama Desert, known as the driest place on earth, which lay partly in Chile, partly in Peru, and partly in Bolivia. Chile challenged its northern rivals for the nitrate fields, and extended its border northwards to take over the desert area, including all the coastal territory that had belonged to Bolivia. Ethnic Bolivians living around the port city of Arica still talk about throwing off the Chilean yoke and getting their country access to the Pacific again.

Winning the War of the Pacific against its northern neighbors made Chile the undisputed power on the west coast of the Americas and generated an economic boom. The nitrate Chile now monopolized was valuable both as a fertilizer and as an ingredient in explosives and munitions. But getting nitrate out of Chile's desert soil required more capital than digging guano had. Chile attracted British investors, and soon joint ventures were shipping a million tons of nitrate per year out of the desert. Production grew steadily until 1914, when World War I created new incentives for Britain's enemies to find an alternative.

Abandoned nitrate-processing station, Atacama Desert, Chile.

Fritz Haber was a German chemist who developed the high-pressure method of extracting nitrogen from the atmosphere that is used today to produce nearly all the nitrogen used in industry and agriculture. Carl Bosch, working for German chemical company BASF, scaled up Haber's laboratory experiment to industrial production. In 1914, BASF produced 20 tons a day for the war effort. Haber and Bosch were each awarded Nobel Prizes for their work in chemistry.

The Haber-Bosch process requires not only high pressures to extract atmospheric nitrogen, but a great deal of energy. About five percent of the world's production of natural gas is required to produce about 500 million tons of ammonia each year. The application of concentrated nitrogen to farm fields increased production even over the yields that had been achieved using guano and nitrate, causing a global explosion in crop yields known as the Green Revolution. By 2010, 133 million tons of ammonia were produced worldwide, about three quarters of which was applied as fertilizer. Corn yields per acre increased fivefold, and other staple crops such as rice saw increases of three or four times. Historian of technology, Vaclav Smil, estimates that if crop yields had stayed where they were in 1900, then by 2000 farm fields would have needed to cover at least half the land on the ice-free continents in order to feed the world's population, instead of the fifteen percent they now occupy. Another way of putting this is that nearly half the people alive today would starve, without the Haber-Bosch process.

Clara Immerwahr, 1870-1915, was a Ph.D. chemist, women's rights activist, and pacifist.

In addition to nitrate, Fritz Haber's other contributions to the German war effort were the chlorine-based chemical warfare agents used against allied troops in World War I and the cyanide-based pesticide Zyklon A, a predecessor of the poison used against prisoners in the concentration camps during World War II. Haber's wife, Clara Immerwahr, the first woman ever to receive a Ph.D. from the University of Breslau, killed herself with her husband's gun when she discovered he had supervised the first successful use of chlorine gas at the second battle of Ypres in 1915. Their son Hermann emigrated to the U.S. and committed suicide in 1946 after discovering that his father's invention had been used to kill millions of their fellow German Jews. Fritz Haber did not live to see Zyklon B used in the concentration camps. He died while moving to Palestine in 1934.

The Haber-Bosch process is not the only way to make nitrogen fertilizer. As mentioned earlier, soil bacteria and symbiotic microbes living on legumes fix nitrogen from the atmosphere. And there are other chemical processes that can be applied on industrial scales. Some of these industrial processes are much less energy-intensive than the Haber-Bosch. For example, a hydro-electric plant in Norway used its surplus energy to make ammonia for fertilizer from 1911 to 1971, using a process developed before Fritz Haber made his discovery. However, almost all the nitrogen used in commercial fertilizer is currently produced through the Haber-Bosch process. As a result, fertilizer prices tend to follow natural gas prices, and ammonia-based fertilizers will probably continue to be made using the high-energy process until energy costs rise substantially.

Uncertainty regarding the reserves of phosphate rock makes phosphorus a strategic mineral followed by global security analysts.

Phosphorus and Potassium

The second element Liebig discovered was crucial to plant growth is phosphorus. Unlike nitrogen, which makes up seventy-eight percent of Earth's atmosphere, phosphorus is a mineral. Traditional agriculture recycled phosphorus by returning manure to fields as fertilizer. During the green revolution, most of the phosphorus applied by the world's farmers has been superphosphate, a concentrate manufactured from a raw material called phosphate rock. Phosphate rock is a sedimentary mixture of minerals deposited in earlier geological eras on the bottoms of ancient oceans. Guano was also rich in concentrated phosphate, and after the Atacama Desert became the main source of nitrates, much of the guano remaining on the Pacific islands was used to produce phosphate fertilizer. The deposits currently used to make fertilizer contain about thirty percent phosphorus.

Although phosphorus is plentiful in the Earth's crust, known deposits of phosphate rock are finite. Estimates of the concentrated phosphorus remaining vary, and depend on assumptions about yet to be developed technologies for discovering and recovering the mineral. Some scientists believe phosphorus production may peak around 2030, and then decline as exploitable reserves are exhausted.

Like nitrogen, inexpensive and plentiful phosphorus has boosted crop yields greatly. Eighty percent of the phosphate rock mined each year goes to produce fertilizer. Phosphorus shortages would create serious threats to world food supply, which would impact global security. But since phosphorus is still available in animal and human waste, a shift back toward applying manures to agricultural fields would greatly reduce demand for superphosphate. Recognizing the growing value of the chemicals contained in our waste, some urban sewage treatment operations have begun producing concentrated phosphorus fertilizers from city sewer sludge.

A modern industrial fertilizer plant.

Potassium, the third major plant nutrient, is actually named after the potash that early American colonists made from trees they burned to clear their fields. Ashes were soaked in water, and then the water was evaporated in cast iron pots to produce lye (potassium hydroxide) and potash (a mixture of potassium chloride and potassium carbonate). Wood ash yielded about ten percent potash by weight, so by clearing a few acres of trees per year, settlers could produce a product they could sell back East for cash. The first patent issued by the United States in 1790 was for a "new apparatus and process" for making potash.

Like phosphorus, commercial potassium fertilizers are manufactured from deposits mined at the sites of ancient inland seas. Current world production is dominated by two cartels, but known reserves total more than three hundred times annual production, so the element is not considered strategic.

Hazards

One of the problems associated with using concentrated soluble nitrogen, phosphorus, and potassium (NPK) in agriculture is that uptake by crops is less than 50 percent. In the old days of ten-foot deep prairie soils, this wouldn't have been a problem. Organic matter binds elemental nutrients, and then decays slowly and releases the chemicals into the soil over many seasons. The deep root systems of perennial grasses stored nutrients in biomass. And the chemistry of organic soils and the microscopic life that thrived in those soils held onto the rest. But in the shallow-plowed fields of modern farms, root systems are not deep enough to catch and hold nitrogen, phosphorus, and potassium as it runs off with the water. And much of the soil life that once thrived in farm fields and pastures has been eliminated by pesticides, herbicides, and fungicides.

The green revolution has been criticized by environmentalists for ignoring the problems created by fertilizer runoff. Excess fertilizer contributes nearly half of the nutrients that are currently poisoning American streams and rivers. Fertilizers entering the watershed encourage algal blooms. The decaying algae traps dissolved oxygen, creating hypoxic dead zones. The dead zone in the Gulf of Mexico has shrunk from its 2002 peak of 8,500 square miles. But excess fertilizer continues to flow down the Mississippi into the ocean.

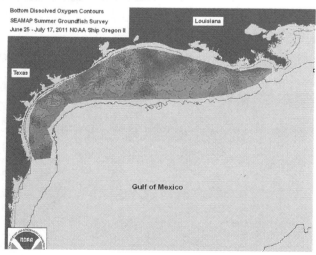

The green revolution has also been criticized by less developed nations for increasing poor people's dependence on technological solutions created in the faraway laboratories and factories in american and other industrialized nations. In many cases, development loans from organizations like the World Bank are tied to spending on products from the donor nations. Critics argue this benefits the donors more than the recipients and puts poor farmers at risk when they become dependent on new technologies and then can't earn enough with their crops to pay rising prices for seeds, fertilizers, and pesticides. Farmers in developing nations have been encouraged with generous loans to invest in expensive capital equipment they cannot afford when the loans disappear. Since the 1990s, more than a quarter million Indian farmers have killed themselves because they can't escape the cycle of debt created by their green revolution involvement in high-tech agriculture.

Dust Bowl

In America, the green revolution that began with the use of guano, potash, and nitrate and accelerated with ammonia, superphosphate, and potassium led to bonanza farming and the extension of agriculture onto marginal lands. The Russian Revolution and World War I at the beginning of the twentieth century reduced European farm production and drove up the price of American grain. Marginal high plains grazing lands like those of western Kansas and Nebraska, Oklahoma and northwestern Texas were put under the plow. Cropland in this region doubled between 1900 and 1920, and then tripled again between 1925 and 1930.

Plowing fields for annual corn and wheat planting is such a common farming practice, it seems normal. On the high plains, perennial grasses had found water deep in the soil and held onto it. Plowing exposed the soil to the sun and wind, and cut the roots that trapped moisture and bound the soil together. And generations of American farmers, taught to depend on plentiful commercial fertilizers, had forgotten the value of hu-

mus. Since Justus von Liebig had focused their attention on soil chemistry in the 1840s, scientists had run with the idea that chemical nutrients were the important thing, and that soil itself was just an inert medium. Although the prairies had been rich in living organic material, the farms built on those original soils relied on imported chemicals rather than nutrients produced by biological activity in the soil. Many farmers even burned off the stems and stalks left after each harvest. Then the soil blew away.

The western edge of the prairie was a different ecosystem from the eastern edge by the Great Lakes, but the change in climate was gradual. Rainfall was scarcer, and the wind blew harder. Between 1933 and 1935, drought struck the area. Actually, dry conditions returned after a few years of unusual wetness that had been taken by hopeful farmers and optimistic boosters as the region's permanent climate. Over half a million people were left homeless when their topsoil blew away.

In a single storm, beginning on November 11, 1933, topsoil from Oklahoma was blown all the way to Chicago, where over 12 million pounds fell on the city like snow. Like alfalfa, guano, and nitrate in the nineteenth century, America's topsoil was blasted from west to east. On Black Sunday, April 14, 1935, dust storms were reported from the Canadian border to Texas. Reporters wrote that they couldn't see five feet through the blowing dust.

The agricultural disaster caused an exodus from the area that became known as the Dust Bowl. But it wasn't just an agricultural disaster. Of 116,000 families surveyed on their way into California, only four out of ten of the refugees were farmers. A third were white collar professionals. When the farms blew away the whole region was wiped out.

Nearly a century later, much of the Dust Bowl region is again under the plow. The wheatfields of Kansas, Texas, Oklahoma, and Colorado produced 411 million bushels of grain in 1933, before the drought began. The Dust Bowl disaster cut production by three quarters, but by 2012, the region was once again growing 700 million bushels of wheat. This time, farmers have taken advantage of irrigation.

The Ogallala is one of the world's largest aquifers, stretching from South Dakota to West Texas. Farmers have been drawing water from it for over fifty years. But the aquifer is not an

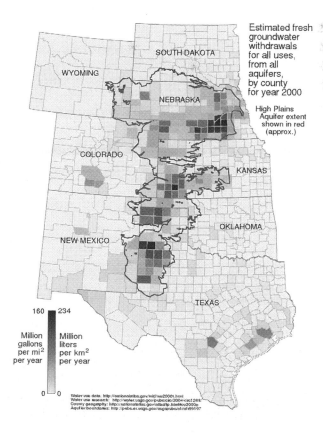

Estimated fresh groundwater withdrawals for all uses, from all aquifers, by county for year 2000

High Plains Aquifer extent shown in red (approx.)

unlimited resource. Sections of West Texas and Kansas have already run out of water, and irrigation is still accelerating. Between 2001 and 2008, farmers used about a third of the water that was taken from the aquifer during the entire twentieth century. If the aquifer is depleted and irrigation becomes impossible on the high plains, American grain production will be reduced by 700 million bushels per year. Farmers will have no choice but to replant perennial prairie grasses and convert the plains back to rangeland, if they are to prevent the soil blowing away again. The question is, will American agribusiness change willingly and thoughtfully before a crisis, or out of desperate reaction once crisis strikes.

Further Reading

Edward Dallam Melillo, *Strangers on Familiar Soil: Rediscovering the Chile-California Connection.* 2015.

Vaclav Smil, *Enriching the Earth: Fritz Haber, Carl Bosch, and the Transformation of World Food Production.* 2004.

Donald Worster, *Dust Bowl: The Southern Plains in the 1930s.* 1979.

Supplement: Questioning triumphalism

Enriching the Earth is a book that has recently been discovered and promoted by billionaire Bill Gates, who says it is one of the best books he's recently read. In it, historian of technology Vaclav Smil identifies the nitrogen-fixing technology of the Haber-Bosch process as the single most important invention of the modern age. Without the cheap, abundant nitrogen fertilizer provided by the process, Smil says, the world population would not have been able to grow from roughly 1.6 billion in 1900 to the current 7 billion plus. Smil does mention that this human population explosion has not been without consequences for the rest of nature, and he notes that the Haber-Bosch process is extremely energy-intensive. If energy shortages drive up the cost of natural gas, the prices of fertilizer and food can be expected to rise with it. But Smil doesn't really explore the question hanging in the air: did global population rise in the last century beyond a level that can be sustained? I imagine this is a question that doesn't seem serious if you believe that energy production and consumption will continue to increase; perhaps changing forms as society transitions from fossil fuels to something new, but never really decreasing. Maybe it's best left to science fiction writers to explore what happens to our modern culture if we lose our access to plentiful, inexpensive necessities like fertilizer and irrigation, if energy becomes scarce or very expensive.

There's little doubt Smil is correct in his claim that at least 40 percent of the people now living owe their continued existence to the cheap fertilizer produced using the Haber-Bosch process. There's also no doubt that issues like quantity vs. quality of life, humanity's impact on the ecosystem, and the distribution of the fruits of progress, which Smil avoids addressing, are valid ones. Maybe another question we ought to ask has to do with the role of Environmental History. Should it be about simply recording the things humans discovered they were able to do, and the positive consequences? Or should it call attention to unintended consequences like the ones Smil avoids, and suggest people think about these questions? Since we continue to develop technologies that allow population to rise, it's a question about the future as well as the past. The way books like *Enriching the Earth* mix the history of science and technology with economic, social, and cultural history creates an interesting opportunity to use environmental history to understand the present and speculate about the future.

In the postscript Smil mentions that in addition to his work on nitrogen fertilizer, Fritz Haber also oversaw the German Chemical Warfare Service. "By the war's end," Smil says, "the casualties of gas warfare amounted to about 1.3 million." So there's definitely a temptation to tell Haber's story as a Faustian tale of the double edged nature of technological progress. Smil chooses not to focus on that interpretation, but he provides readers with all the details necessary to draw their own conclusions.

Bibliography

This is a small assortment of books you could read to learn more about the material covered in this text. It's a *small sample* of the many interesting books available on Environmental History and other branches of history and the sciences that influence this growing field. For more suggestions, and to see what I'm reading, visit my blog at EnvHist.net.

Sven Beckert, *Empire of Cotton, A Global History*. 2014.

Colin G. Calloway, *New Worlds for All: Indians, Europeans, and the Remaking of Early America*. 2013.

Christopher Clark, *The Roots of Rural Capitalism*. 1990.

William Cronon, *Changes in the Land: Indians, Colonists, and the Ecology of New England*. 1983.

William Cronon, *Nature's Metropolis: Chicago and the Great West*. 1991.

Alfred W. Crosby, *The Columbian Exchange: Biological and Cultural Consequences of 1492*. 1972.

Benita Eisler, ed., *The Lowell Offering: Writings By New England Mill Women (1845-1940)*. 1997.

Clive Finlayson, *The Humans Who Went Extinct: Why Neanderthals Died Out and We Survived*. 2010.

Susan E. Gray, *The Yankee West: Community Life on the Michigan Frontier*. 1996.

Morton Horwitz, *The Transformation of American Law, 1780-1860*. 1977.

Bill Kovarik, "Henry Ford, Charles Kettering and the Fuel of the Future," *Automotive History Review*, Spring, 1998. Available online at www.environmentalhistory.org

Marc Levinson, *The Box: How the Shipping Container Made the World Smaller and the World Economy Larger*, 2006.

Charles C. Mann, *1491: New Revelations of the Americas Before Columbus*. 2005.

Charles C. Mann, *1493: Uncovering the World Columbus Created.* 2011.

Edward Dallam Melillo, *Strangers on Familiar Soil: Rediscovering the Chile-California Connection.* 2015.

David J. Meltzer, *First Peoples in a New World: Colonizing Ice Age America.* 2009.

Shawn William Miller, *An Environmental History of Latin America.* 2007.

Matthew Parker, *The Sugar Barons: Family, Corruption, Empire, and War in the West Indies.* 2012.

Charles Postel, *The Populist Vision.* 2007.

Malcolm Rohrbough, *The Land Office Business: The Settlement and Administration of American Public Lands, 1789-1837,* 1968.

Malcolm Rohrbough, *The Trans-Appalachian Frontier,* 2008.

Joel Salatin, Folks, *This Ain't Normal: A Farmer's Advice for Happier Hens, Healthier People, and a Better World.* 2011.

Upton Sinclair, *The Jungle.* 1906.

Vaclav Smil, *Creating the Twentieth Century: Technical Innovations or 1867-1914 and their Lasting Impact,* 2005.

Vaclav Smil, *Enriching the Earth: Fritz Haber, Carl Bosch, and the Transformation of World Food Production.* 2004.

Ted Steinberg, *Nature, Incorporated.* 1991

George Rogers Taylor, *The Transportation Revolution, 1815-1860,* 1977.

Donald Worster, *Dust Bowl: The Southern Plains in the 1930s.* 1979.

Index

Appendix: Image Sources

All the images in this text are copyright free. Most are from online sources such as Wikipedia and the Library of Congress, and are either:

- Covered by a creative commons license,
- Copyright expired, or
- In the public domain because they were created by a government worker.

Some are images I acquired myself in archives and got permission to use.

Format: Image Name, Source name if any, Source url.

Introduction

Earth from space
NASA/Apollo 17
https://en.wikipedia.org/wiki/Earth#/media/File:The_Earth_seen_from_Apollo_17.jpg

Chapter One

Americas Earth
Martin23230
https://en.wikipedia.org/wiki/Americas#/media/File:Americas_%28orthographic_projection%29.svg

Skull
Didier Descouens
https://commons.wikimedia.org/wiki/Category:Prehistoric_human_skulls#/media/File:T%C3%A9viec_Crane_Profil_Droit_II.jpg

Landing of Columbus
John Vanderlyn
https://en.wikipedia.org/wiki/File:Landing_of_Columbus_%282%29.jpg

Evolutionary Tree
Chris Stringer
https://en.wikipedia.org/wiki/File:Homo-Stammbaum,_Version_Stringer-en.svg

Ice Age Temperature
Robert A. Rohde
https://en.wikipedia.org/wiki/File:Ice_Age_Temperature.png

Glacier
https://en.wikipedia.org/wiki/File:Perito_Moreno_Glacier_Patagonia_Argentina_Luca_Galuzzi_2005.JPG

Sea Level
Robert A. Rohde
http://globalwarmingart.com/wiki/File:Post-Glacial_Sea_Level_png

Clovis Point
https://en.wikipedia.org/wiki/Clovis_point#/media/File:Clovis_Point.jpg

Smilodon
Wallace63
https://fa.wikipedia.org/wiki/%D9%BE%D8%B1%D9%88%D9%86%D8%AF%D9%87:Smilodon_head.jpg

Hebior Mammoth
MCDinosaurhunter
https://commons.wikimedia.org/wiki/File:Hebior_Mammoth_Clean.png

Teosinte
John Doebley
https://en.wikipedia.org/wiki/Zea_%28genus%29#/media/File:Maize-teosinte.jpg

Manioc
David Monniaux
https://en.wikipedia.org/wiki/File:Manihot_esculenta_dsc07325.jpg

Mesa Verde Cliff Palace
Gustaf Nordenskiöld
https://en.wikipedia.org/wiki/Mesa_Verde_National_Park#/media/File:Mesa-Verde---Cliff-Palace-

in_1891_-_edit1.jpg

Tenochtitlán
https://en.wikipedia.org/wiki/Age_of_Discovery#/media/File:Tenochtitlan_y_Golfo_de_Mexico_1524.jpg

Andean Terraces
Alexson Scheppa Peisino
https://commons.wikimedia.org/wiki/File:Pisac006.jpg

Marajoaran Burial Urn
https://en.wikipedia.org/wiki/Marajoara_culture#/media/File:Burian_urn,_AD_1000-1250,_Marajoara_culture_-_AMNH_-_DSC06177_b.jpg

Chapter Two

Columbus Map
https://en.wikipedia.org/wiki/Christopher_Columbus#/media/File:ColombusMap.jpg

Newfoundland Map
Coach.nyta
https://en.wikipedia.org/wiki/L'Anse_aux_Meadows#/media/File:Newfoundland_map.png

Skálholt Map
Sigurd Stefánsson
https://commons.wikimedia.org/wiki/Category:Sk%C3%A1lholt#/media/File:Sk%C3%A1lholt-Karte.png

Old Greenland Map
Emanuel Bowen
https://commons.wikimedia.org/wiki/Category:Old_maps_of_Greenland#/media/File:Old_Greenland_1747.jpg

Atlantic Cod
https://en.wikipedia.org/wiki/Atlantic_cod#/media/File:Atlantic_cod.jpg

Columbus Notes to Marco Polo
https://en.wikipedia.org/wiki/The_Travels_of_Marco_Polo#/media/File:ColombusNotesToMarcoPolo.jpg

Mercator 1569 Map
https://en.wikipedia.org/wiki/Mercator_1569_world_map#/media/File:Mercator_1569.png

Mercator Projection Map
Strebe
https://en.wikipedia.org/wiki/Mercator_projection#/media/File:Mercator_projection_SW.jpg

Gall-Peters Projection
Strebe
https://en.wikipedia.org/wiki/File:Gall%E2%80%93Peters_projection_SW.jpg

Voyages of Columbus
Phirosiberia
https://en.wikipedia.org/wiki/File:Viajes_de_colon_en.svg

Red Jungle Fowl Hen
JJ Harrison
https://commons.wikimedia.org/wiki/Gallus_gallus#/media/File:Gallus_gallus_female_-_Kaeng_Krachan.jpg

Smallpox Virus
CDC/ Dr. Fred Murphy; Sylvia Whitfield
http://phil.cdc.gov/phil/details_linked.asp?pid=1849

Florentine Codex
Bernardino de Sahagún
https://en.wikipedia.org/wiki/File:FlorentineCodex_BK12_F54_smallpox.jpg

Triple alliance
El Comandante
https://en.wikipedia.org/wiki/File:Aztec_Empire_1519_map-fr.svg

Cinchona
Franz Eugen Köhler
https://commons.wikimedia.org/wiki/File:Cinchona_calisaya_-_K%C3%B6hler%E2%80%93s_Medizinal-Pflanzen-179.jpg

Potosí
Pedro Cieza de León
https://en.wikipedia.org/wiki/Potos%C3%AD#/media/File:Capitulo-CIX.jpg

Castas painting
https://en.wikipedia.org/wiki/Casta#/media/File:Casta_painting_all.jpg

Chapter Three

First Thanksgiving
Jean Leon Gerome Ferris
https://en.wikipedia.org/wiki/Thanksgiving_%28United_States%29#/media/File:The_First_Thanksgiving_cph.3g04961.jpg

Treaty of Tordesillas
https://en.wikipedia.org/wiki/Treaty_of_Tordesillas#/media/File:Treaty_of_Tordesillas.jpg

St. Augustine
https://upload.wikimedia.org/wikipedia/commons/d/db/Mapstaug.jpg

Map of Virginia
Captain John Smith
https://en.wikipedia.org/wiki/File:Capt_John_Smith's_map_of_Virginia_1624.jpg

Gulfstream map
Benjamin Franklin

https://en.wikipedia.org/wiki/Gulf_Stream#/media/File:Franklingulfstream.jpg

New Amsterdam
John Wolcott Adams, Isaac Newton Phelps Stokes
https://en.wikipedia.org/wiki/Castello_Plan#/media/File:Castelloplan.jpg

Turkeys
Dan Allosso

Indian Village
Theodor de Bry
https://en.wikipedia.org/wiki/Theodor_de_Bry#/media/File:Indian_Village_of_Pomeiooc_Theodor_de_Bry_1590.jpg

Indian Village
John White
https://en.wikipedia.org/wiki/Secotan#/media/File:North_carolina_algonkin-dorf.jpg

New Netherlands
Willem Blaeu
https://en.wikipedia.org/wiki/New_Netherland#/media/File:Blaeu_-_Nova_Belgica_et_Anglia_Nova.png

Three sisters
United States Mint
https://en.wikipedia.org/wiki/Three_Sisters_%28agriculture%29#/media/File:2009NativeAmericanRev.jpg

Cod overfishing
http://sciencelearn.org.nz/Contexts/The-Noisy-Reef/Sci-Media/Images/Collapse-of-the-cod-fisheries

Purchase of Manhattan
Alfred Fredericks
https://en.wikipedia.org/wiki/Peter_Minuit#/media/File:The_Purchase_of_Manhattan_Island.png

Metacomet
Paul Revere
https://en.wikipedia.org/wiki/Metacomet

Map of Caribbean
https://en.wikipedia.org/wiki/Antilles#/media/File:Carte_antilles_1843.jpg

Virginia Tobacco Slaves
https://en.wikipedia.org/wiki/File:1670_virginia_tobacco_slaves.jpg

Chapter Four

Ohio Territory
https://en.wikipedia.org/wiki/South_and_East_of_the_First_Principal_Meridian

Proclamation Line

Kooma
https://commons.wikimedia.org/wiki/File:Map_of_territorial_growth_1775.svg

Ohio River Map
George Washington
https://en.wikipedia.org/wiki/George_Washington#/media/File:Washington_Pennsylvania_Mapb.jpg

US 1789 Map
Golbez
https://ja.wikipedia.org/wiki/%E3%83%95%E3%82%A1%E3%82%A4%E3%83%AB:United_States_1789-08-1790-04.png

Ordinance grid diagram
Isomorphism3000
https://en.wikipedia.org/wiki/Land_Ordinance_of_1785#/media/File:1785_Land_Ordinance_Diagram.jpg

Gannett population maps
Scanned from 1910 Census

Old Growth Forest
Snežana Trifunović
https://en.wikipedia.org/wiki/Old-growth_forest#/media/File:Biogradska_suma.jpg

Log House
George-Henri-Victor Collot
https://archive.org/details/journeyinnortham-12coll

Colonel John Wayles Jefferson
https://en.wikipedia.org/wiki/John_Wayles_Jefferson

Trail of Tears map
https://en.wikipedia.org/wiki/Trail_of_Tears#/media/File:Trails_of_Tears_en.png

Erie Canal
W. H. Bartlett
https://en.wikipedia.org/wiki/Erie_Canal#/media/File:Lockport_bartlett_color_crop.jpg

Alonso Franklin Ranney
Photo from archives

Hillsdale County map
Photo from archives

Bridget O'Donnell
Illustrated London News
https://en.wikipedia.org/wiki/Legacy_of_the_Great_Irish_Famine#/media/File:Irish_potato_famine_Bridget_O%27Donnel.jpg

Enfield Massachusetts
Photo from archives

Henry Sears Ranney
State of Massachusetts congressional Photos
http://archives.lib.state.ma.us/handle/2452/203656

1880 map of Allen Michigan
Photo from archives

Ranney Letters
Photos from Ashfield Historical Society archive

Chapter Five

Grist Mill
Dudesleeper
https://en.wikipedia.org/wiki/Gristmill#/media/
File:Wayside_Grist_Mill.JPG

Warren Bridge
Celebrate Boston
http://www.celebrateboston.com/map/boston-map-1838.jpg

Shad
Sherman Denton
https://en.wikipedia.org/wiki/American_shad#/
media/File:Dentonshad1904.jpg

Atlantic salmon
Timothy Knepp
https://en.wikipedia.org/wiki/Atlantic_salmon#/
media/File:Salmo_salar.jpg

Fish trap
https://en.wikipedia.org/wiki/Shad_fishing#/media/File:Pedee_detail.jpg

Mount Vernon
George W. Boynton
https://en.wikipedia.org/wiki/George_Washington#/media/File:A_Map_of_Washington%27s_
Farms_at_Mt._Vernon_%281830_engraving%29.
jpg

Freshet
Jean Philippe Richard
https://en.wikipedia.org/wiki/Freshet#/media/
File:Ouareau_jps0029.jpg

New Lanarck
Photo from archives

Lowell Mill
J. E. Rice
http://www.personal.psu.edu/jkh185/blogs/lowell_mill_girls-_cmlit_107/Lowell%20Mill%20
Map.jpg

Factory Girls
National Child Labor Committee
http://www.loc.gov/pictures/item/ncl2004000962/
PP/

Factory Girl
Lewis Hine
https://en.m.wikipedia.org/wiki/Lewis_Hine#/
media/File%3AHine%2C_Lewis%2C_Adolescent_Girl%2C_a_Spinner%2C_in_a_Caroli-

na_Cotton_Mill%2C_1908.jpg

Merrimack River
Karl Musser
https://en.wikipedia.org/wiki/Merrimack_River#/
media/File:Merrimackrivermap.png

Lowell Mills 1900
Detroit Publishing Co.
http://www.loc.gov/item/det1994001463/PP/

Slater Mill
Dougtone
https://en.wikipedia.org/wiki/Slater_Mill_Historic_Site#/media/File:Pawtucket_slater_mill.jpg

Lowell Canal system
Mark M. Howland, Margy Chrisney
https://en.wikipedia.org/wiki/History_of_Lowell,_Massachusetts#/media/File:1975_map_of_canal_system_in_Lowell,_Massachusetts.png

1836 Constitution
Factory Girls Association
https://en.wikipedia.org/wiki/Lowell_Mill_Girls#/
media/File:FGA_Constitution.jpg

Lowell Bleachery
Sifney & Neff
https://en.wikipedia.org/wiki/Timeline_of_Lowell,_
Massachusetts#/media/File:1850_bleachery_Lowell_Massachusetts_detail_of_map_by_Sidney_and_
Neff_BPL_11051.png

Pemberton Mill
Frank Leslie's Newspaper

Chapter Six

Promontory Point
Andrew J. Russell
https://en.wikipedia.org/wiki/Transcontinental_railroad#/media/File:East_and_West_Shaking_hands_at_the_laying_of_last_rail_Union_Pacific_Railroad_-_Restoration.jpg

Whiskey Rebellion
Frederick Kemmelmeyer
https://en.wikipedia.org/wiki/Whiskey_Rebellion#/
media/File:WhiskeyRebellion.jpg

Postroads
Personal scan of census documents

Pittsburgh
Samuel W. Durant
https://en.wikipedia.org/wiki/File:Pittsburgh_1795_
large.jpg

Battle of New Orleans
Kurz and Allison
https://en.wikipedia.org/wiki/Battle_of_New_Orleans#/media/File:Battle_of_New_Orleans,_January_1815._Copy_of_lithograph_by_Kurz_and_Al-

lison,_published_1890.,_ca._1900_-_1982_-_
NARA_-_531128.tif

Erie Canal
https://en.wikipedia.org/wiki/Erie_Canal#/me-
dia/File:Erie-canal_1840_map.jpg

Clermont
Detroit Publishing Co.
https://en.wikipedia.org/wiki/North_River_
Steamboat#/media/File:Clermont_replica.jpg

New Orleans route
Kmusser
https://en.wikipedia.org/wiki/New_Orle-
ans_%28steamboat%29#/media/File:Neworle-
ans_steamboat_route.png

Tom Thumb
R. J. Machett
https://en.wikipedia.org/wiki/Tom_Thum-
b_%28locomotive%29#/media/File:Steam_En-
gine_-_an_ad_in_Matchetts_Baltimore_Direc-
tor_1831.jpg

Travel Time
Personal scan of archival text

Abraham Lincoln
Abraham Byers
https://en.wikipedia.org/wiki/Abraham_Lin-
coln#/media/File:Abraham_Lincoln_by_
Byers,_1858_-_crop.jpg

Illinois Central Land Grant
Personal scan of archival material

Railroad Land Grants
1880 US General Land Office Map

George Custer
https://en.wikipedia.org/wiki/George_Arm-
strong_Custer#/media/File:Custer_Staghounds.
jpg

Great Northern Map
Poor's Manual of Railroads
https://commons.wikimedia.org/wiki/File:1897_
Poor's_Great_Northern_Railway.jpg

Waterloo Boy
Newspaper Ad
http://ag-museum.com/wp-content/up-
loads/2011/10/Waterloo_Boy_Tractor_Ad.jpg

Interstate Map
SPUI
https://en.m.wikipedia.org/wiki/File:Map_of_
current_Interstates.svg

Ford Model T
Harry Shipler
https://en.wikipedia.org/wiki/Ford_Model_T#/
media/File:1910Ford-T.jpg

Standard Oil Octopus
Udo Keppler
https://commons.wikimedia.org/wiki/File:Stan-

dard_oil_octopus_loc_color.jpg

PA Oil Field
https://en.wikipedia.org/wiki/Pennsylvania_oil_
rush#/media/File:Earlyoilfield.jpg

Ethyl Ad
https://images.search.yahoo.com/yhs/search;_
ylt=A0LEV7jrzEhWIDAAoIsnnIlQ;_ylu=X-
3oDMTByMjB0aG5zBGNvbG8DYmYxBHB-
vcwMxBHZ0aWQDBHNlYwNzYw--?p=Eth-
yl-Gasoline-Ads-from-the-1950s&fr=yhs-mozil-
la-002&hspart=mozilla&hsimp=yhs-002

Ethyl trademark ad
http://www.environmentalhistory.org/billkovarik/

Container Port
Calvin Teo
https://en.wikipedia.org/wiki/Port_of_Singa-
pore#/media/File:Port_of_Singapore_Keppel_
Terminal.jpg

Chapter Seven

Poland Pig
http://www.bbqsuccess.com/berkshire-pork/

Cincinnati 1841
Klauprech & Menzel
https://en.wikipedia.org/wiki/Cincinnati#/media/
File:Cincinnati-in-1841.jpg

Pork Packing
Harper's Weekly
http://www.loc.gov/pictures/item/2004677270/

Ice Harvesting
https://en.wikipedia.org/wiki/Spy_Pond#/media/
File:Spy_Pond_Ice_Harvesting_from_a_1854_
print.jpg

Retail Cuts of Beef
http://www.ansi.okstate.edu/resources/upload-
ed_files/b-wcutsofbeef.jpg/view

Refrigerator Car
http://www.cs.mcgill.ca/~rwest/wikispeedia/
wpcd/images/212/21250.jpg.htm

Union Stockyards
https://en.wikipedia.org/wiki/File:Livestock_chi-
cago_1947.jpg

Stockyards
https://en.wikipedia.org/wiki/The_Jungle#/
media/File:Chicago_stockyards_cattle_pens_
men_1909.jpg

Floor Workers
Suhling & Koehn
https://en.wikipedia.org/wiki/The_Jungle#/
media/File:Floorers_removing_the_hides_USY_
Chicago_%28front%29.tiff

Chicago Tinned Meat
http://www.archives.gov/exhibits/whats-cooking/
preview/factory.html

Meat Inspection
H.C. White Co.
https://en.wikipedia.org/wiki/The_Jungle#/
media/File:Chicago_meat_inspection_swift_
co_1906.jpg

Lumber
Photo from archives

Sears Magnolia House
https://en.wikipedia.org/wiki/Sears_Catalog_
Home#/media/File:Sears_Magnolia_Catalog_Im-
age.jpg

Chicago Lumber District
Harper's Weekly
http://www.encyclopedia.chicagohistory.org/
pages/3030.html

Peshtigo Fire
http://www.majordojo.com/images/WER2002-
07a.jpg

Minneapolis Mill District
Frank Pezolt
https://en.wikipedia.org/wiki/Mills_Dis-
trict,_Minneapolis#/media/File:MillsDis-
trict-MPLS-1895.jpg

Political Cartoon
https://img.4plebs.org/boards/pol/im-
age/1434/23/1434235805551.jpg

Mary Elizabeth Lease
https://en.wikipedia.org/wiki/Mary_Elizabeth_
Lease#/media/File:Mary_Elizabeth_Lease.jpg

USDA Stamp
Government work, public domain

Guano
https://en.wikipedia.org/wiki/File:D-
SCN5766-guano-glantz_crop_b.jpg

Nitrate oficina
https://en.wikipedia.org/wiki/Humberstone_
and_Santa_Laura_Saltpeter_Works#/media/
File:Humberstone.jpg

Clara Immerwahr
https://en.wikipedia.org/wiki/Clara_Immer-
wahr#/media/File:Clara_Immerwahr.jpg

Fertilizer Plant
Sharon Loxton
https://en.wikipedia.org/wiki/Haber_process#/
media/File:Severnside_fertilizer_works_-_geo-
graph.org.uk_-_189990.jpg

Phosphorus
Wilson44691
https://en.wikipedia.org/wiki/Phosphorite#/me-
dia/File:Phosphorite_Mine_Oron_Israel_070313.
jpg

Gulf Dead Zone
NASA/NOAA
https://en.wikipedia.org/wiki/File:Dead_Zone_
NASA_NOAA.jpg

Dust Storm 1935
NOAA George E. Marsh Album
https://commons.wikimedia.org/wiki/File:-
Dust-storm-Texas-1935.png

Dallas, SD
USDA
https://en.wikipedia.org/wiki/File:Dust_Bowl_-_
Dallas,_South_Dakota_1936.jpg

Chapter Eight

Elevator
Canadian Plains Research Center
http://esask.uregina.ca/entry/grain_elevators.
html

Wheat
Katya Swarts
https://zh.wikipedia.org/wiki/File:Wheat-haHu-
la-ISRAEL2.JPG

Great Plains map
https://en.wikipedia.org/wiki/File:US_Great_
Plains_Map.svg

Alfalfa
Amédée Masclef
https://en.wikipedia.org/wiki/Alfalfa#/media/
File:75_Medicago_sativa_L.jpg

Made in the USA
Lexington, KY
03 August 2017